Candy, Chocolate, Ice Cream,
and How to Lick 'em!

For Mom and Dad
with Love and Hershey Kisses

By the authors of
I Haven't a Thing to Wear!

The *On/Off Diet* Book for Everyone
Who Loves to Eat
Hates to Diet
and Wants to Stay Slim Forever!

Candy, Chocolate, Ice Cream and How to Lick 'em!

by
SANDY SPRUNG

with
Judith Keith

Tandem Press, Tannersville, Pa.,
Lester and Orpen, Toronto

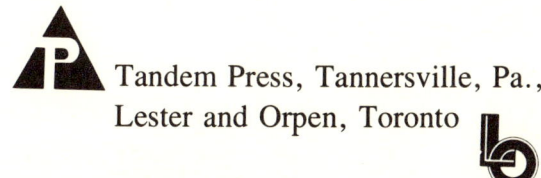

Copyright © 1973 by Sandy Sprung
All rights reserved. No part of this book may be reproduced in any manner whatsoever without written permission of the publisher, except for brief quotations embodied in critical articles and reviews.

Library of Congress Catalog Number   73-78887

ISBN Number   0-913204-02-3

Printed in the United States

"Life's a banquet and most poor sons of bitches are starving to death!"

Auntie Mame by Patrick Dennis

"Life's a banquet and most poor sons of bitches are dieting!"

Sandy Sprung

Thank you Judith Keith, my good friend and collaborator.

Robert Shapiro, M.D., for your professional suggestions concerning the psychiatric aspects of this volume.

Stanley Title, M.D., specialist in the field of obesity, for your professional assistance.

Liz Koch Feder, B.S. in Food and Nutrition, Member of the American Dietetic Association, for your professional knowledge in the fields of nutrition and home economics.

Roy Weiss, my legal advisor.

And a special thank you, Daniel Rosenwein, for your editorial assistance and moral support.

Contents

Foreword *ix*
Introduction—Eat but be Thin! *xi*
 1. The *Obesie* and the *On/Off Diet* 1
 2. Scorpio with Fat Rising 6
 3. The Yo-Yo Syndrome 13
 4. Food as a Drug, Fat as an Excuse 17
 5. Discovering North America and the *On/Off Diet* 24
 6. Climax! 30
 7. Getting Down to Getting Down 36
 8. On the *On/Off Diet* 45
 9. A Brand New Habit 53
10. Off the *On/Off Diet* 57
11. Freud and Food 66
12. Living it Up While Taking it Off 69
13. Healthful Eating and the *On/Off Diet* 75
14. Menus and Recipes 83

The Candy, Chocolate, Ice Cream and
How to Count 'em Calorie Counter 107

Foreword

Fat or thin, actress or housewife, Sandy Sprung has always possessed a tickling and incisive humour which she has retained... despite her 100-pound weight loss. In this book, at first glance "light and frothy," she has uniquely combined some sound and fundamental psychological concepts related to obesity with an innovative, refreshing, and practical approach to the daily plight of the obese and/or "obese-prone" individual. Imagine being permitted *two* martinis at one sitting and still losing weight! The vast problem of controlling obesity has been approached from many vantage points. Chief among these have been the superficial dietary approach or some form of psychotherapy. As a practicing psychoanalyst, I, naturally, lean toward the latter as an effective process to understand the basis for exorbitant food needs. The usual dietary regimes—too often accompanied by fistfuls of multicolored pills as an adjunct—lead to only temporary results and impose harsh restrictions upon one's daily life.

Sandy, in essence, insists upon both psychological insight *and* a weight-loss diet with the essential ingredients of fun and freedom. I commend her attempt at apprising the *obesie* of what may be "going on inside" as well as what to "take inside."

This funny-serious volume should be of help to all who face weight problems, but of immeasurable value to those who desire to enjoy and participate in the greater freedoms which characterize our contemporary society and its attendant life styles. I suspect Sandy's point of view emerged as a solution to a rather typical dilemma of how a girl with a good appetite can be sated and smashing simultaneously! Her *On/Off Diet* presents an approach permitting one to taste all of life . . . at least every other day!

Robert S. Shapiro, M.D.,
Associate in Psychiatry,
Psychoanalytic Clinic for Training
and Research,
Columbia University.

Introduction

Eat but be Thin!

Our world revolves not around the sun, but around the table! In Western civilization we have always tended to equate the pleasure of success with *Food*. The head of the family is the *breadwinner who brings home the bacon* or *dough* or *bread*. When he knows whom *to butter up*, he's successful and has *everything from soup to nuts*. If he knows *which side his bread is buttered on*, he also *takes the cake* and for him *life is just a bowl of cherries*.

Food measures the pain of our disappointments as well. If we *count our chickens before they hatch* we may be *dropped like a hot potato* and wind up with *sour grapes* which may be our *just desserts*!

In today's society eating for pleasure has become more than a symbol of well-being. The joy of eating is practiced, preached, exulted, verily venerated in the thousands of thirty and sixty second sermons which are delivered via the channel of your choice.

The great god *Food* is further glorified through the pulpits of print. In supermarket-shrines throughout the land, altars are heaped high with offerings of almost unlimited variety.

If the ancient Jews had worshipped *Food* the way we do now, the Ten Commandments would not have been handed down to Moses on tablets of stone, but on tablets of Alka Seltzer!

Most of us have learned our catechism well. Our new-found god at times even replaces the God of our fathers, or runs Him a close second. People seem to attend more church suppers than church services, more bar mitzvah dinners than bar mitzvahs. The *Joy of Cooking* is runner-up to the Bible in world-wide sales!

"Corpulence is next to Godliness" chant disciples as they gain in number and in weight. Eating, once merely a national pastime now transcends into a religious experience!

And then, just as America is uplifted pound by pound and all but totally converts, a new messiah appears on the mount preaching yet another gospel: "Thin is In! Thin is In!" and a modern crusade begins.

On one side are the legions of manufacturers, vendors, advertisers of comestibles—ubiquitous, unflinching, bombarding the populace with electronic and engraved images of their god *Food*.

Opposing them are massed a vociferous army of doctors, insurance actuaries, nutritionists, cardinals of fashion, the "beautiful people"—all prosletysing "The Wages of Sin Are Fat! Repent Disbelievers! Renounce thy strawberry cheesecake chocolate seven layer cake lobster newburg lasagna stroganoff Mom's apple pie! Convert to bouillon cubes, celerey stalks, and diet soda!"

One High Priestess of the "New Thin" declares "wine and wafer are not *legal*." What to do for Communion? "Matzoh is not *legal*." What to do at Passover? In her cult, guilt must be felt, penance must be paid, confession must be heard! "Forgive me, Mother, for I have eaten!"

xii

Where there was once only pleasure there is now pain. Paradise has been lost and the forbidden fruit—and cakes and candies—seem that much sweeter!

I was caught in the middle, my allegiance torn between the two camps. I would feast over a weekend. All I could hear was "Eat But Be Thin! Eat But Be Thin!" with every mouthful. The weight of my transgressions was so great that I would stagger into the opposing camp and purge myself in the cleansing waters of starvation until the voice faded away.

Then one glorious day my conflict was resolved! The *On/Off Diet,* the Dove of Piece appeared. It promised a piece of candy, a piece of cake, and above all, peace of mind. A truce was drawn, resolving the way I love to eat and the way I love to look and feel. The truce has set me free and the truce shall set you free too—free from pain, free from guilt, and free to enjoy your life.

1

The *Obesie* and the On/Off Diet

I am an actress by profession and an *obesie* by habit. Looking at me now you would never guess that at one time eating was my life. I didn't consume food. It consumed me. I used to think that I was doomed to an *obesie* way of life because I was born with my sun in Scorpio, moon in Taurus, and fat in Thigh!

I used to weigh 246 pounds. Now I carry 140 pounds on a 5'9" frame, wear a size 12 dress, often go bra-less, and always go girdle-less. That's because I am now a controlled *obesie*.

I answered "yes" to the following questions. Do you?

- Are you a member of "The Piece Corps," never leaving a piece on your plate because people are starving in India?
- Are you a human garbage pail? When they step on your toe does your mouth open?
- Are you so full you can't put another morsel in your mouth? But you do—like a hot fudge sundae!
- You have money in the bank, but do you constantly wonder where your next meal is coming from?

- Do you drop weight one month and then soar to new heights the next, like the Jolly Green Yo-Yo?
- When it comes to cookies, chips, or pretzels, does eating "just one" mean just one box?
- When Sir Edmund Hillary was asked why he climbed Mt. Everest, he replied, "Because it's there." Do you eat food for the same reason?
- When you see yourself in a bathing suit, do you pray for rain?
- Is being fat the only thing that makes you miserable and is eating the only thing that cheers you up?
- Is every day the day before you start your diet?

If you answer "yes" to most of these questions then you too are an *obesie*. What's an *obesie*? The word is not in the dictionary. It's in the mirror and it's in your mind.

An *obesie* is a person whose avocation is eating, whose hobby is losing and gaining weight. (In the time I've wasted thinking about food I could have become a concert pianist!)

I use the term *obesie* because it is so close to *junkie*. The *obesie*'s drug is food. He is hooked on food for many of the same reasons an addict is hooked on drugs or an alcoholic on liquor.

I bet you are saying, "Oh, I'm not an *obesie*. I don't eat *that* much!"

That's exactly what the alcoholic says about liquor. "I don't drink that much!" He is not aware that he drinks excessively because no alcoholic drinks a bottle all in one gulp. He hides the 100 proof of his self-delusion with a martini or two at lunch, two martinis or three with dinner and sips, sips, sips all evening long. If he actually counted up all he drank in just one day, he'd be shocked.

The woman who "doesn't eat that much" invariably has

"nothing" for breakfast, except, or course, the leftover cereal, egg, toast, and jelly from the kids' breakfast (300 calories); has "nothing" for lunch, except, of course, a "few" slices of pizza and two cokes (800 calories) while out marketing; a "tiny" dinner (800 calories) plus all the remains of the pot roast, potatoes, and gravy on the serving plate (1,000 calories) and "only black coffee" with half of a "small" pecan pie (900 calories) before going to bed. This woman who "doesn't eat that much" put away 3,800 calories in one day! The daily calorie quota for the average woman varies from 1,500 to 2,000 calories per day, depending on her age, bone structure, and the weight she would like to be.

The man who "doesn't eat that much" has a donut at coffee break (250 calories), two martinis and a "handful" of nuts (1,500 calories) before a "diet" lunch (1,000 calories); drinks and hors d'oeuvres (2,000 calories) before dinner (2,000 calories) and "some" pretzels, cheese, and beer (1,000 calories) while watching television. His total for that day was 7,750 calories. His calorie quota should vary between 2,600 and 3,300!

Perhaps *you* are not aware that you *do* eat that much. If you carefully counted *all* the calories of *all* the food you ate in just one day would you be shocked? Try it! Could you then honestly say "I don't eat that much"?

Nor do you have to be 50 or 100 pounds overweight to be an *obesie*. Perhaps it is only an extra ten pounds that *constantly* plague you. *All you need to qualify is a chronic hassle keeping your weight where you want it.*

The closer the *obesie* gets to the table, the further he gets from his goals. The more compulsively he eats, the greater he and his problems become. His life is one vicious circle—himself.

I was that vicious circle. My first thought each morning was: "Today I'm really going to diet!" My last thought each night was: "Tomorrow I'm really going to diet." In between was a series of: "I shouldn't be eating this but..."

For twenty years I clung to crash diets, clutched at diet pills, gritted my teeth. I even contemplated sewing up my mouth, all in an attempt to lose weight. Everything worked, but only for a while. Why?

I was merely treating the symptoms of obesity, not its causes. I needed insight to uncover the reasons for my overeating and to effect a permanent change in my eating habits.

But insight comes slowly and in spurts. While we are inching our way toward self-awareness, how do we control ourselves from barrelling our way up the scale?

In non-*obesies*, control is provided by a smoothly operating will power and *appestat*—a traffic signal that unconciously regulates the amount of food non-*obesies* eat so that they unthinkingly maintain their Ideal Weight. If the *obesie's* appestat and will power were in good shape, he would be too.

We *obesies* need appestat and will power transplants! But until science has developed this kind of operation we must rely on an eating program that will substitute for both. *We need a program that is varied enough so that we do not have to overtax our weakened will power. We need a program that will act as an appestat so we know when we have had all the food required to maintain our Ideal Weight.*

But because most *obesies* are not at their Ideal Weight (When was the last time you saw your Ideal Weight grinning up at you from your bathroom scale?), *this same program has to be a reducing program as well.*

Pretty fat order! If I had known all those years what I

was looking for I would have said it was impossible to find. Only after I stumbled onto the On/Off Diet while on tour with the musical comedy, *Mame*, did I realize it was the perfect diet for *obesies*.

The On/Off Diet provides precisely what we *obesies* crave—*Food*, all kinds of food, even fun food like ice cream, pizza, and french fries—*while you lose weight*. As you lose, you develop new eating habits which will help you maintain your Ideal Weight indefinitely. At last you can have your cake and figure too!

The dynamic duo of insight and the On/Off Diet made me slim and has kept me slim for the first time in my life. If it works for an *obesie* like me, it will work for *anyone*, even for those who are convinced that they are not *obesies*!

If you would do anything to be slim, except give up the foods you love to eat, then this diet and this book are for you!

2

Scorpio with Fat Rising

I began life November 13 of an undocumented year. I weighed 5 pounds, 15 ounces, normal by most standards but a cause for concern in my family where food wasn't nourishment—it was oxygen!

"She's so skinny!"

"Is she sick?"

"What kind of a mother are you?"

Only poor relations were skinny! In a society where "bulk is beautiful," I was doomed. Within a year my mother had corrected my birth "defect." Home movies of my first party show a blown-up, pudgy cherub, too busy eating the icing on her birthday cake to blow out the candles.

My fondest childhood memories are food-filled: Sunday family dinners in New York's Chinatown at Hang Far Low's; lobster feasts at Lundy's in Sheepshead Bay hosted by my grandfather; Saturday afternoons at the movies, sucking B-B Bats (Do they still make them?) and after the show collecting all the change in my pockets to buy a Charlotte Russe at the corner candy store. For me, where there was fun there was always food.

Every night after dinner the family would all race out to the local drive-in—for ice cream, not movies! We did this with such regularity that the owner of the stand named my mother "Mrs. Chocolate." Like the conscientious bartender at your favorite watering spot, our ice cream man would start setting up the family's "usuals" when he saw us getting out of the car. If we were late he would wait for us before cleaning out the chocolate machine for the night. If we were to miss an evening, Mother would call him to explain. After all, she didn't want him to worry!

At seven I was a 75-pound roly-poly and a budding *obesie* devouring everything in sight, in whatever quantity was available. I remember eating five pounds of peanut brittle at one sitting. Why five pounds? That's how much was in the box!

By the time I was nine the die was cast, the table set. I didn't know it then, but I had become a full-blown *obesie*. (Ninety-five pounds is very full!) Even then, although I was ashamed of my excessive eating, I was helpless to stop it. What I was doing to myself was a crime!

> THE FILE OF SANDY SPRUNG, NEE SONDRA SCHNEIDER—CRIMINAL AT VERY LARGE. FREQUENTS CANDY STORES, BAKE SHOPS, ICE CREAM PARLORS. ARMED WITH FORK, KNIFE, SPOON, AND STRAW. DISTINGUISHING CHARACTERISTIC: *FAT*.

Subject's First Misdemeanor—"The Candy Caper:" Visiting friends bring box of chocolates to family. Later same night after all are asleep subject carefully opens box, eats most of candy, removes incriminating empty wrappers and spreads remaining candy around in box in attempt to disguise theft. Subject rewraps, ties, and replaces box in pantry. Following day, unknowing family visits father's boss bringing same box of candy. Parents utterly chagrined when box is opened revealing half of contents missing!

Age 10—125 pounds: Subject attempts getaway after mother enforces first diet. Flees to Camp Sequoia where macaroni salad, noodles, potatoes, bread, and pancakes are served daily. Subject also runs up highest canteen bill in camp's history!

Age 11—138 pounds: Takes it on the lam—and corned beef and pastrami by holing up in Florida with Aunt Beck, Queen of the Sandwich Makers.

Age 14—161 pounds: First boy friend, Seymour, breaks up with subject after hysterical scene in ice cream parlor. When questioned, Seymour reported, "I don't understand it. She was always such a quiet, sweet girl. But when I refused to buy her a third sundae, she went nuts!" Subject pleaded temporary insanity. "I couldn't help it," she wailed. "Blame it on my banana split-personality!"

Age 15—180 pounds and still rising: Sent to New York Reform School, the Dubarry Success Course. Temporary rehabilitation. Loses 40 pounds in six weeks. Released at 140. Returns to old haunts and old habits. Gains 10 pounds in ten days.

While other kids were growing up, I was growing out: out of "Chubby" sizes and out of half sizes. By the time I was Sweet Sixteen I was into maternities. Yes, I wore a maternity outfit to a friend's party because it was the only attractive formal we could find to fit me.

By the time I was eighteen, diets were my thing. Other girls were out dancing, I was home dieting. Other girls were counting karats, I was counting calories. And the health spas I had been to could fill an entire Sunday *New York Times* resort and travel section. There wasn't a diet I hadn't had under my belt.

At twenty-three I started to work for the "Mrs. America Contest" as Executive Coordinator. I set up personal appearances for the titleholder in different cities throughout the country. I arranged and attended breakfasts, luncheons, cocktail parties, and dinners given by the sponsors of the contest at which "Mrs. America" officiated. In Chicago, as she addressed herself to the invited guests, I addressed myself to the menu. In New Orleans, we were entertained on a riverboat. As we cruised the Mississippi, I cruised the creole. At every turn "Mrs. America" was feted and I was fatted. In Las Vegas, while others waited for the slot machines to throw three lemons, I waited for the candy machines to throw Three Musketeers. In Fort Lauderdale, someone called "breaktime!" Before he could mouth "hot coffee and donuts," I drooled "Yes!" and downed six cups of coffee and nine donuts. "Mrs. America" began to eye me with alarm. During the five years I worked for the contest I gained 50 pounds.

I became the "Downhill Racer" of the Fat Set. On crash diets my weight would plummet at a breakneck speed of 8 to 12 pounds the first week. A month or two later I would arrive at an acceptable base, exhausted, ravenous, totally spent from my ordeal. An avalanche of food followed. I couldn't shovel it in fast enough. Soon I was atop a new peak, huffing, puffing, gasping for breath, waiting until I could gather enough determination for my next downhill run.

When I was offered the position of Assistant Director of Public Relations of the International Automobile Show, I thought, "Great! How could I get fat from fenders!" Easy!

10 / Candy, Chocolate, Ice Cream and How to Lick 'em!

There were always food-filled festivities given for or by the exhibitors. At one of them I met a dynamic Detroit ad man and we dated. I didn't see him again for two years. During that time I gained 40 pounds. We accidentally ran into each other at a cocktail party and he gave me a quizzical but friendly smile. "You look so familiar," he said. Suddenly he beamed and exclaimed, "Why, of course, the last time I was in town I dated your kid sister!"

Those were the years I discovered the only real difference between a spinster and a swinger *is* 40 pounds!

When I met my husband I weighed 165, though that was thin by my standards. During our courtship, in order to stay at that weight I constantly downed diet pills. The day he proposed I stopped taking them. By our wedding day, not only had I gained a husband, I had gained 30 pounds!

Our first apartment was furnished in "Early Refrigerator." I cooked for two but shopped for four and ate the two extra portions while preparing the meal. Did it kill my appetite? What appetite? I never had an appetite, but I always wanted to eat and eat and eat and eat!

My husband, a rugged sportsman, turned me onto the great outdoors and to the wonders of nature. We hiked, we golfed, we skiied, we sailed. No. That's not quite right: he hiked, I stayed at the campfire and toasted marshmallows for breakfast; he golfed, I gulped at The Nineteenth Hole; as he climbed higher and higher on glaciers, I got higher and higher on gluwein!

Once, while I was waiting for him to finish a run, a young skiier approached me, asking:

"Where did you find a place to go horseback riding around here?"

"What makes you think I'm going riding?"

"The pants you're wearing."

"My pants? They're custom-made stretch ski pants."

The boy answered with all the honesty of youth, "Oh, I thought you were wearing jodhpurs!"

I really hit my stride the year we bought a sail boat. Everyone at the boathouse ran around in little white ducks. I was the 200-pound duck who waddled around in a huge white housedress because I couldn't find slacks to fit me. One day when we were out sailing on Long Island Sound, we had just rounded a marker and I went forward to cleat a line. Just then the wind blew up. My housedress and I billowed in the breeze. At that moment another boat came along side and someone yelled,

"Ahoy there, your spinnaker's come undone."

(For those of you unfamiliar with sailing, a spinnaker is a huge balloon-like sail.)

"Ahoy there, yourself," my husband replied, "that's no spinnaker, that's my wife!"

One morning at 3 a.m. I was starving. Of course I was starving—I hadn't eaten a thing since midnight. I crept into the kitchen and quietly opened the refrigerator door. I was just about to dig into a leftover noodle pudding when I felt my husband's hand on my shoulder.

"Sandy, Sandy, dear, what are you doing? You just started a new diet."

"What am I doing?" I fired back in innocent indignation. "What does it look like I'm doing? I'm defrosting the refrigerator!"

Some girls get kissed in the kitchen. I used to get caught!
Oh! The excuses I made up:
"I only ate the jelly because I needed the empty jar."

"Didn't you know that after a heavy meal Tootsie Rolls cut the grease!"

When I was really trapped once with a corned beef sandwich between my teeth, I just smiled coyly and said, "I don't want to get *too* thin." At the time I weighed 210!

One night as my husband popped into the shower, I popped into the refrigerator for some chocolates to munch while reading in bed. He emerged from the bathroom unexpectedly. Not wanting him to catch me eating, I quickly hid the chocolates in the top of my nightgown. I thought I would eat them later, after he went to sleep. But he didn't want to go to sleep! I never dreamed those chocolates would plague me *during*. My husband snapped on the light and snapped off my head.

"What the hell is this?" he cried, his face and hands smudged with chocolate. "When are you going to stop eating?"

"Why are you angry with me?" I fired back. "You're the one who's been nibbling!"

3

The Yo-Yo Syndrome

By laughing at my own expanse, I was truly laughing at my own expense. I refused to take my overweight seriously and therefore I couldn't do anything serious about it. I made fat jokes about myself, perhaps to insure that no one else would. Like so many other "jolly" fat people, with food-in-cheek, I masked the pain I was really feeling.

I soon gained a reputation as a funny fat lady and was asked to co-author a musical for our community center. It would take a great deal of my time and I wondered if my husband would object.

"Honey, are you kidding?" he beamed. "Anything that keeps you out of the kitchen is just fine with me!"

The musical was a huge success. Encouraged by its response, I felt if I could make people laugh for fun, perhaps I could make them laugh for profit. I contacted nightclubs, comedians, and industrial producers and soon began to sell original material to a revue here, a comic there, a trade show here and there.

One day I auditioned sketches for a Broadway producer who said, "Oh, you're a performer as well as a writer!" I melted. Figuratively right then, and literally during the next six weeks when I lost 35 pounds. That one remark had started my motor-vation running. At last I was hooked on something other than *Food*—performing. I enrolled in acting classes, started taking vocal lessons, bought the show business trade papers for possible jobs, but most important, I started and stuck to a diet. I began to realize that all roads do not lead to the refrigerator. My first professional audition was for Charles Nelson Reilly who was directing a revue. To my utter delight I got a part.

That was soon followed by some Off-Off-Broadway and Off-Broadway work. While appearing in the revival of Gershwin's *Of Thee I Sing*, I read in the trades that touring companies of the Broadway musical *Mame* were being cast. I hungered for the role of Vera Charles, "the first lady of the American Theater" who is Mame's bosom friend. But how could that flamboyant and chic actress be played by the me who was still searching for stylish stouts at Lane Bryant's?

My first audition for Mr. John Bowab, who has directed more companies of *Mame* than any other man on this planet, was a total disaster. He thought I was trying out for the role of Mame's mother-in-law, a grotesquely corpulent woman! I knew if I were ever to be considered for the part of Vera, I would have to be thinner. I wavered off my diet not one nibble.

A few months later I re-auditioned for Mr. Bowab. This time I read for the part of Vera Charles but the word was that I was "not physically right for the role." (A nice way of saying I was too fat!) Undaunted, I continued to diet. Just the prospect of playing Vera was enough to keep me on the straight and narrower.

Thirty pounds later when an agent asked me if I had ever auditioned for the role of Vera, I lied through my teeth (clenched from dieting) and said, "No!" I prayed Mr. Bowab wouldn't recognize me because of the weight I had lost. He didn't and he hired me to play Vera in the summer tour starring Miss Edie Adams.

But the moment I got the job I began to eat compulsively again. My theatrical star was on the rise and so was my weight. You'd think that the fulfilment of my wish would whittle my weight away; that once my career had begun to blossom I would no longer have the need to binge; that if my horizons were expanding my hips wouldn't. But I had a little bit too much for lunch, a little bit too much for dinner, and much too much at night, until my overeating accelerated and exploded into familiar *obesie* orgies.

I flew from New York to our engagement in Washington, D.C. On the plane lunch was served—"toy food." Had I not been air sick I would have been ravenous. At a party that night, thank Bacchus, I was able to sit up and take a little nourishment. I downed six glasses of champagne, a dozen canapes, tons of cold cuts, and globs of celebration cake. In the publicity photographs you can almost watch me gaining weight!

Judas sold his soul for thirty pieces of silver. I sold my figure for thirty-one flavors of ice cream. Thirty-one—count 'em—thirty-one, that not only defied description, they defied dieting. It was during that summer I met and fell in love with Mr. Baskin and Mr. Robbins. The tour was on the "Straw Hat Circuit," but I was doing two-a-day at Baskin-Robbins Ice Cream Parlors. (What I thought was only a summer caprice with Messrs. Baskin and Robbins was to develop into a sweet relationship which still continues to enrich my life!)

In Washington, I ordered not a cone, not a sundae, but an entire store! I rented a Baskin-Robbins store for an after-the-show party for the cast and crew, inviting them to come dressed as kids. Edie wore a huge bow in long moppet curls, a pinafore and patent-leather "Mary Janes." Our musical director came dressed as Charlie Brown. One of the chorus girls asked if she could come in just a diaper. It would have been the first X-rated Baskin-Robbins in America! Outside the store in the parking lot, we rollerskated, blew bubbles, played hopscotch, tag, and other childhood games. Inside I acted like a kid too and made a childhood fantasy come true: to run rampant through an ice cream parlor, tasting as many combinations of flavors and toppings as my imagination and digestive system would allow.

I licked and slurped and sucked and mouthed and twirled and swallowed and gulped and gorged all thirty-one flavors heaped high with whipped cream, hot fudge, butterscotch, marshmallow, sprinkles, bananas, nuts, and cherries. Wow!!

How much did this little party cost me? Not much, only 8 pounds—overnight!

I was struck with terror and again it was D-Day: dull, dreary, dismal, depressing day after day after day of denial and drastic dieting. I was bored, cranky, felt sorry for myself and I hated everyone who was eating what I couldn't eat. At that time to diet was to die!

I was once more caught up in the Yo-Yo Syndrome, that too familiar pattern of going up the scale, then down the scale, then up and down and up again, and I was miserable!

Would I ever be able to reconcile the way I wanted to eat with the way I wanted to look or would I always ride that ridiculous rollercoaster of weight loss and gain and loss and gain?

I have to diet to live the life I love, but how to live with dieting?

4

Food as a Drug Fat as an Excuse

I knew there were many more thin roles than fat ones. I knew I was more attractive slim. I knew all the statistics about obesity usually shortening life. And yet, except for occasional crash diets, I could not stop overeating!

One dawn of the week the summer tour with *Mame* ended, I was watching the movie *A Hatful of Rain* on television. The film is about a young, married man, ostensibly normal, but who is a drug addict. As I sat in the darkness devouring an enormous piece of cake, I unconsciously said outloud, "He needs his fix and I need mine."

The sound of my own voice startled me and I was astounded by the sharp edge of insight which had cut through to my consciousness. I was so stunned I even stopped eating!

Was I an addict too? The comparison scared the hell out of me. As a junkie thinks only of *smack*, I thought only of snacks. As a junkie shoots up with a needle, I shoveled in with a spoon. As an alcoholic falls off the wagon, I fell into the refrigerator.

"Why, I am a food addict. I am an obesie!"

This stunning bolt of insight was just the beginning of my

understanding why I overate and what role fatness played in my life. This awareness did not spring forth all at once. It flowed from my unconscious to my conscious in tiny streams and it still does. Insight starts with a crumb of an idea, then a speck of association until it slowly grows into huge chunks of self-understanding. Gradually, over the next two years, this is what I learned about myself:

FOOD WAS OUR FAMILY'S SYMBOL FOR LOVE, REWARD, PUNISHMENT (GOODNESS AND BADNESS), CONCERN. It was filled with implied values and meaning.

Food as Love. In part, my pattern of obesity was set by years of Mother's love, served on a silver platter heaped high with hugs, kisses, and extra portions.

Food as Reward. I remember my parents saying "You're a good little girl. You can have more ice cream." To this day I *adore* ice cream. Whenever I eat it, unconsciously am I Daddy's good little girl again?

Food as Punishment. "You're a bad girl. You can't have any dessert." Perhaps the reason I never passed up dessert was that not having it made me feel as though I had done something wrong!

Food and Concern (all in one gulp). "Have something to eat, you *look* hungry!" "The last spoonful on the plate has all the goodness in it. Besides, don't you want to belong to the Clean Plate Club?" It seemed like such an ingroup that I licked my plate dry and became the club's most *outstanding* member.

FATNESS AS MY TECHNIQUE TO SATISFY STRONG NARCISSISTIC CRAVINGS. I wanted to be someone special, to be noticed, and my overweight did this for me. I literally stood out in a crowd. My fatness was my identity. I was "that fat girl" and later "that fat lady." It even gave me a special position in my family of fatties where it seemed as though we had weight-gaining contests. I was *always* the winner! Whenever I would lose 30 or 40 pounds my friends would "oh" and "ah" and the limelight was bright. Going up the scale and down, then up and down, up and down, assured me of my place in center stage. People noticed when I gained weight but they rarely commented—that would have been impolite. However, I remember once my girl friend's Freudian slip showing. She had not seen me for a year during which I had gained 40 pounds. She greeted me, "Sandy, you're a sore sight for eyes." It was negative attention, but it was attention. I was the ball of the ball!

SLIMNESS AS THE "IMPOSSIBLE DREAM." While others worked toward building a successful business or legislating against social injustices or establishing hospitals in Africa, my life's work, my ultimate goal, was to be thin. As Stuart Byron said in his *Village Voice* article, "The Unmaking of a Fattie," "A true commitment to social action is almost impossible for the obese. One considers oneself fat before one considers oneself Jewish or black or homosexual or a woman. Personal liberation for him is the first order of business." For me there was really very little else other than not being fat. If I became slim and stayed slim, I wondered what in life I would have to accomplish, to champion, to look forward to.

FATNESS AS A MEANS OF PROCRASTINATION. How many times I said, "When I'm thin, I'm going to _____" (fill in your own word). I imagined that if I were slim I would be more productive, more successful, more everything. If I were no longer fat what excuse would I have for not accomplishing all the things I claimed I wanted to do. Never being thin for more than ten seconds, it was easy to put off doing all the things I planned.

OBESITY AS AN UNCONSCIOUS DEFENSE AGAINST SEXUAL FEARS. When I was an adolescent, sex scared me. The fatter I became, the less attractive I was to boys and later men, which saved me from many anxious situations.

FOOD AS IMMEDIATE PLEASURE. I had little ability to sustain discomfort and so I "acted out" my needs with food. There was a direct line from the market to my mouth. I ate food straight from its package. My excuse was I didn't want to dirty a plate. My real reason was I couldn't wait because there is nothing more immediate than the pleasure of food to satisfy those screaming, unconscious demands:

"I'm frustrated and eating makes me feel good *now*!"
"I'm lonely and eating makes me feel good *now*!"
"I've failed and eating makes me feel good *now*!"

Even, "I'm so disgusted about being *fat* that eating makes me feel good *now*." As ridiculous as it may seem, I remember trying on a bathing suit and being so depressed at the way I looked that I left the shop and immediately gobbled a hot fudge sundae!

FOOD USED TO HIDE MY ANGER. I became furious when I didn't get what I wanted from the world. To compensate for this lack of "feeding," I fed myself instead. In addition to being hostile, I couldn't openly express this hostility for fear of rejection. I would stuff food in to hold back the fury I was too insecure to release. My eating binges were the equivalent of other people's temper tantrums.

FOOD AS A TRANQUILIZER AND BUFFER AGAINST INSECURITY AND ANXIETY. I was an excellent student, but always quite anxious about the way I would fare in exams. I remember cramming for finals while cramming myself with food. Studying made me less ignorant and stuffing made me less anxious. The combination resulted in my graduating at the top of my class and at the top of my scale.

At parties, rather than make the first move toward strangers, I would move toward the refreshments. I wasn't a wallflower, I was a buffet-blossom!

I didn't realize it then, but the summer I first performed in *Mame* was a period of great anxiety for me. I was in a major role, playing opposite a star, and I was comparatively inexperienced. The day rehearsals started I met the principal members of the cast. They were all veteran actors and very close, having just worked together in another company of *Mame*. I hadn't even been shown the staging and they had been doing the show for over a year! Did I feel insecure and out of it! I wandered away from the group, across to the other side of the theater, a huge summer tent, and plopped down next to the youngster who was playing Mame's ten-year-old nephew. I felt he would be the least threatening of the cast. Darrell smiled, said "Hi!", looked around, sighed, and said, "God, it's been *years* since I've played a tent!"

I was just plain scared and I did what any other *obesie* does when tension and anxiety and doubt and fear mount: I calmed myself with my own home remedy, my own brand of tranquilizer, *Food*.

If some of your personal experiences parallel mine, if you have a chronic problem with 10 or more pounds, if you use food as a drug and fat as an excuse, then you too are an obesie. Only when you accept this as fact will you begin to gain insight into the real cause of your overeating.

Overeating has been your way of living with pressure and anxiety. It has been your pattern and it will take time to change. Don't be impatient! Don't expect immediate changes in your way of thinking about yourself or in the manner in which you cope with your problems. During this period of adjustment rely on the *On/Off Diet* so that as you are gaining insight you are also losing weight. *Introspection and the On/Off Diet will effect a permanent change in your eating habits.*

The trip down the scale is a bitch! It takes effort and exploration, but it can be done! Some people may require professional help in order to become more introspective. I believe you will find therapy is neither as frightening nor as expensive as you might think.

The next time you want to eat and you know the desire has nothing to do with the body's need for fuel, instead of saying, "I'm starved," ask yourself, "What do I really want?" Are you upset, angry, anxious, frustrated, depressed? Do you feel unloved, unappreciated, or un-whatever? What are the circumstances surrounding your feelings?

For every excuse you have for overeating there is a better reason not to. I once asked my husband if he loved me more when I weighed less. He, being very nice, said he loved me the same. Well, for years I used that as a convenient cop-out. Whenever I wanted to binge I would rationalize, "It doesn't matter how fat I get. My husband likes me this way." Then I realized that if his love remained constant as my weight went down, he would be loving me *more per square inch*!

If you feel a compulsion to binge, try very hard at that moment to ask yourself what it is you might unconsciously want. You may not stop yourself entirely but you could lessen the binge's length and intensity. After a binge, don't beat yourself with a guilt-edged thrasher. You will only feel worse and want to eat more. Question yourself instead. Do you binge at certain times? Do you binge with certain people? As your insight grows, so will your will power!

It's imperative we get to the crux of our problems, because the nearer to the truth we come, the closer to the bone we'll stay!

5

Discovering North America and the *On/Off Diet*

Toward the end of the summer tour I was signed to repeat my role of Vera Charles in the national company of *Mame* starting that fall. It was to play throughout the United States and Canada for ten months, first starring Sheila Smith, then the marvelous Annie Russell, and later the divine diva, Miss Patrice Munsel. Along that route I discovered a diet—*the diet*—the *On/Off Diet!*

ON it I reached my Ideal Weight!
OFF it I stayed at my Ideal Weight!
Best of all, I ate all the foods I love!

Because self-awareness had added a new dimension to my dieting, heightened insight and the *On/Off Diet* created a dynamic duo which changed my eating habits and my life!

The *On/Off Diet* was not revealed to me in a vision, but, during the tour, as we traveled mile after mile after mile, I began to inch my way down the scale, pound after pound after pound.

The night we opened in Hartford, Connecticut, I weighed 60 pounds more than Sheila Smith, a slender shaft of a woman who is the same height as I. The "S.S. *Mame*" seemed to be listing—to my side and the critics in some of the towns noticed. They reviewed my tonnage as well my talent.

The Dayton Daily News reported I looked "pudgy."

Lawrence DeVine, drama critic, *Detroit Free Press*, said I resembled "Joan Bennett of the Green Bay Packers."

I began downing diet pills to shed the pounds that were up-staging me. But the pills made me so nervous that I did the opening number hanging from the lights by my fingernails. I tossed the pills into the wings, expecting my figure to exit with them. You can imagine my surprise a month later when Emmett Weaver of the *Birmingham Post-Herald* called me "a striking brunette." Then Hannah M. Motiska of the *Scranton Tribune* called me "statuesque."

What was going on? Could the reviewers be astigmatic? Finally, in Phoenix, I had a hotel room with a scale. I jumped on it. It didn't shriek "Fat, Fat, Fat!" It cooed 158!

Could it be that the symbol of the Phoenix and its myth of rebirth was actually coming true for me? Was I really being reborn *thin without dieting?* I had stopped myself from serious binging many times along the tour, which accounted for my not *gaining* weight. But how could I be *losing* weight without actually trying—without starving myself? Truly it was a miracle! There could be no other explanation.

Then one rainy afternoon I was skimming through my pocket diary to recall some unusual sight or happening that I could relate in a letter to a friend. I was amused to see that although my daily notations included museums, historic landmarks, and places of geographic interest, most of my comments were detailed accounts of meals in each and every town we played. A monument might go by unnoted but not a steak and certainly never a soufflé!

To my amazement my diary reported a fascinating sequence

of events. It detailed a definite *duality* in my eating habits, revealing some apparent reasons for my mysterious weight loss.

On matinee days I was rushed: I would awaken just in time to go to the theater for the afternoon show. Between performances we would have only a short break. Because I don't like to eat hurriedly or heavily before performing, I would have a light snack in my dressing room. After the show, since restaurants in many of the towns closed early, we had the time, but not the place to eat.

We traveled by bus almost every other day and on these days, because I'm prone to motion sickness and allergic to Dramamine, I ate very little. I had to remain completely inert. The only way to stay motionless in a gypsy caravan crawling with performers' pets and "pet" performers was to sleep. I became known as "The Bus Zombie." I slept from Hartford to Vancouver, back to the Mexican border, up the Eastern seaboard and woke up only for performances, stopovers, and border inspections. *Why, I even slept through meals!*

Therefore, without thinking about it or planning it, on these matinee and travel days I was eating very little.

But then there were days when I was off the bus, off the stage, and off visiting delightful cities and savoring their regional delicacies:

Savannah—"Y'all mean y'all gonna leave without tastin' our Black Bottom Pie at the Pirates' House? Honey, it's the oldest building in Savannah and the best pie in the Confederacy!" Absolutely right! The building was old and the pie to die! *Toronto*—Lobster cardinale, lobster baked with a bit of cheese, herbs, and heaven, followed by banana cream pie that would have made Chiquita proud! *Albuquerque*—Luncheon in Old Town at the quaint La Placita specializing in authentic Mexican food. The tang of the tacos, the tingle of the tamales, olé! *Vancouver*—With the second largest Chinese community in North America and more egg rolls per square inch than downtown Shanghai. Peking duck, chicken and snow peas in blackbean sauce, and mandarin lobster. *Oklahoma City*—A spectacular midnight supper after the show. Iced Mumm's champagne, succelent Chicken Kiev, salad richly laced with roquefort. Cool, cool creme de menthe parfaits, eaten while the restaurant rotated silently, circling the city twinkling and winking itself to sleep. *San Francisco*—Caviar, shrimp and cheese, quenched by double martinis in iced, stemmed glasses, sizzling steaks broiled in butter, steamy baked potatoes plump with sour cream and chives; Caesar salad, verdant leaves glistening with aromatic oil and delicate slivers of anchovies topped with croutons—crunchy, crunchy, so crunchy.

But in spite of all these culinary delights, I lost weight! How could it be possible?

Prior to the tour, the pattern of my eating had been lose then gain, lose then gain; starve then stuff; a week on a diet, a weekend of gorging; three weeks on diet pills, two months binging. During the tour, however, something was different in my eating habits because I was steadily losing, losing, losing.

I had analyzed *why* I overate. Now I decided to analyze exactly *what* I was eating to see if there was some formula for my continuing weight loss. I began to explore what my diary had only hinted at.

Suddenly the tour turned into a scientific expedition! I went to the nearest drugstore to buy a small food scale and a bathroom scale. If the Ancient Mariner could carry the albatross, if Atlas could carry the world, then I, Sandy Sprung, could carry my scales and, of course, my calorie counter! In the past a calorie counter had been around mostly to annoy, chastise, and convict me, but now it was to become my indispensible aide and ally—my Tonto, my Dr. Watson, my Alice B. Toklas! Each morsel of food that touched my tongue was checked and accounted for! I dissected each item on the menu: for its weight, contents and preparation. Is it broiled? Has it butter? Just how much? And from what udder?

This is what I learned:
My life was still one of extremes in terms of my eating habits, but now it had developed into a consistent pattern—one day I ate almost nothing, the next day I ate the kinds of food I wanted. One day I was ON a diet, one day OFF.

On my *On Diet* days I had been eating less than 1,000 calories.

On my *Off Diet* days I had been eating about 2,000 calories.

Every diet I had ever been on suggested that to *lose* weight I should have no more than 1,650 calories per day and to maintain my Ideal Weight I should have no more than 2,100 calories per day. *Therefore, unintentionally, I had been dieting one day and maintaining my Ideal Weight the next!*

I had found a way to lose weight while forming a new habit. Could this new habit enable me to become a *controlled obesie?*

The excitement of my possible discovery made me tremble. At that moment I identified with Albert Einstein the night he must have said to himself in the privacy of his Princeton study:

"$E = Mc^2$ . . . I think!"

I too was converting matter into energy!

I felt like an astronaut (astronette?) for I too was conquering space—my own. I was taking a tiny step for me, a giant leap against obesity!

6

Climax!

Between Phoenix and Denver the *On/Off Diet* changed from theory to fact. In those intervening two and a half weeks of the tour I lost four more pounds by adhering to the principles of the *On/Off Diet*.

On On Diet days I ate 900 calories or less.

On Off Diet days I ate no more than 2,100 calories. (How you determine your own personal *ON Diet* day and *Off Diet* day Calorie Quotas is explained in detail in the following chapter.)

Even 670 calories can be interesting, filling, and nutritious if they are well-budgeted. Here's a sample of an *On Diet* day:

Breakfast

1 orange	60
Granola, 1 oz. (natural cereal)	135
with 4 oz. skimmed milk	45
Coffee, black, no sugar	0
TOTAL	240

Lunch

Fresh fruit cup, 1 cup	100
Cottage cheese, 1/2 cup	100
Coffee, black, no sugar	0
TOTAL	200

Dinner

Red Snapper, 4 oz., broiled, no butter	95
Large green salad with diet dressing	50
Yellow wax beans, 1/2 cup	15
Cantaloupe 1/2	60
TOTAL	220

After the show

| Diet soda and good conversation | 10 |
| DAILY TOTAL | 670 |

On this program dieting was so easy! Who can't suffer through salad with diet dressing and broiled fish without butter when you know dinner the following night could be stuffed clams, duck l'orange, and crepes suzette! *The promise of more food tomorrow helped me get through the diet of today.*

The following day, the Off Diet day, I ate no more than 2,100 calories. It was such a feast compared to the previous day of restraint.

Here's what I had one *Off Diet* day when some of the cast and I went sightseeing. No one suspected I was dieting. Would you?

Breakfast

Cantaloupe 1/2	60
Grilled cheddar cheese, 1 oz.	100
two slices whole wheat bread	110
Coffee, black, no sugar	0
TOTAL	270

Lunch

Chili con carne, 1 cup	300
2 saltines	30
1 apple	80
Coffee, black, no sugar	0
	TOTAL 410

Dinner

1 Martini, extra dry	200
Shrimp cocktail with sauce	100
2 pork chops	350
Red cabbage, 1/2 cup	75
Red wine, 1−4 oz. glass	100
1 dumpling (there were two, one was enough)	80
Salad with 1 T Dressing	150
Layer cake with icing	155
	TOTAL 1210
	DAILY TOTAL 1890

(with plenty of calories leftover in case the chef's hand was heavy)

And I enjoyed this kind of feasting every other day! But the *creme de la creme* was stepping on the scale after that week to find another pound missing!

Of course, there were times when I was tempted to go over my daily calorie quota. Questioning *why* I wanted to overeat was of great value to me. On *Off Diet* days I could not use the excuse that I was *physically* hungry. After all, I had consumed 2,100 calories which certainly was enough fuel for me. Therefore, I knew that my desire for food was psychological and I probed deeper in order to understand what it was that I was really longing for.

On tour I would always reserve some calories for after the show "conversation and munch time." (I, like most actors, are revved up following a performance and need a few hours to unwind.) One night in San Antonio I had already consumed the last of my 2,100 daily calorie quota when someone called to tell me he had just learned that the best Mexican restaurant in town, Mi Tierra, was open all night. Some of the cast were taxiing there and asked if I wanted to go along. I screamed "SI! Si!", grabbed my purse and raced for the elevator as though I hadn't eaten in days. As I was riding down to the main floor I asked myself, "What are you doing? You're not even hungry!" "Oh, yes, I am. I'm starving!" I argued. "But how could you be, you've already eaten 2,100 calories today." Even *I* couldn't fight me with that argument. I realized what I really wanted was not to miss any of the *action*. By the time I reached the lobby I had decided to go along... for the fun, but not for the food. Thanks to the On/Off Diet, the food I could have... as the Mexicans say... *mañana*.

It has been proven that rest periods make it possible to function longer and more efficiently. That is why there is a coffee break in offices, "take five" at rehearsals, and "time out" during games. I was able to stay on the On/Off Diet as long as it took me to reach my Ideal Weight because *half the time it seemed as though I wasn't really dieting.*

Nothing was forbidden, nothing was *illegal*, nothing was sinful, nothing was fattening as long as it did not *exceed* the number of calories I was permitted for that day. Now I no longer felt guilty about eating cake, ice cream, peanut butter, spare ribs, fudge, and you name it. They were all part of my diet! As a matter of fact, these delights were necessary *Off Diet* day fare to bring my calorie count up to 2,100. It couldn't be done on lettuce and celery stalks alone!

> *On Diet days I lost weight!*
> *Off Diet days I maintained my Ideal Weight!*

(How you determine your own personal Ideal Weight is explained in detail in the following chapter.)

Four weeks later on February 14th, in Topeka, the *On/Off Diet* presented me with the most glorious Valentine gift I had ever received: my Ideal Weight!

As I stood on my scale I trembled in utter pleasure: 140 pounds! Then I trembled in utter terror. I had taken the weight off, but I had lost weight many times before. The question now was: could I keep it off and for how long? Or would this be just another case of: "The diet was successful but the patient got fat!"

Not this time! *The Off Diet days trained me to eat correctly, to eat only what I required to maintain my Ideal Weight.* In the future, to stay as slim as I was now, I would continue to eat *every day* as I had been eating on the *Off Diet* days.

> *The On/Off Diet helped me painlessly reach my Ideal Weight!*
> *The On/Off Diet helped me painlessly learn new eating habits!*
> *Therefore, I could painlessly maintain my Ideal Weight!*

Six weeks after Topeka, my Ideal Weight still intact, the *Times-Picayune* of New Orleans reported, "Miss Sprung... is either a look-a-like for a *slimmer* Jane Russell or a younger Joan Bennett." (Italics the author's.) Three weeks later a review in the Newport News, Va. *Morning Press*: "Miss Sprung... is something of a knockout on stage. She's tall with raven black hair and *every curve in the right place*." (Italics the author's.)

For the first time in my life, I have been able to *maintain* my Ideal Weight for more than two minutes. I have done it for more than two *years*. Insight and the On/Off Diet have taught me how to have my *Candy, Chocolate, Ice Cream and How to Lick 'em too*—and so can you!

7

Getting Down to Getting Down

(Before embarking on this or any other diet it is wise to check with your physician.)

Here is how to make the *On/Off Diet* work for you.

Remember the basic principles of the *On/Off Diet:*

> *On Diet* DAY Eat no more than 900 calories and lose weight.
> *Off Diet* DAY Eat no more than your Caloric Quota and maintain your Ideal Weight.

What is your Caloric Quota? What is your Ideal Weight? The following explains these in detail.

YOUR IDEAL WEIGHT. The chart opposite indicates minimum to maximum weight for females dressed, wearing two inch heels, and for men, dressed, wearing shoes. If you weigh yourself nude, women subtract two pounds; men subtract four pounds. Subtract one pound for each year under twenty-five.

Getting Down to Getting Down / 37

FEMALE

IDEAL WEIGHT CHART

HEIGHT (with shoes)	SMALL FRAME	MEDIUM FRAME	LARGE FRAME
4 ft. 10 in.	92- 98	96-107	104-119
4 ft. 11 in.	94-101	98-110	106-122
5 ft. 0 in.	96-104	101-113	109-125
5 ft. 1 in.	99-107	104-116	112-128
5 ft. 2 in.	102-110	107-119	115-131
5 ft. 3 in.	105-113	110-122	118-134
5 ft. 4 in.	108-116	113-126	121-138
5 ft. 5 in.	111-119	116-130	125-142
5 ft. 6 in.	114-123	120-135	129-146
5 ft. 7 in.	118-127	124-139	133-150
5 ft. 8 in.	122-131	128-143	137-154
5 ft. 9 in.	126-135	132-147	141-158
5 ft. 10 in.	130-140	136-151	145-163
5 ft. 11 in.	134-144	140-155	149-168
6 ft. 0 in.	138-148	144-159	153-173

SHOWS MINIMUM TO MAXIMUM WEIGHTS

Courtesy, Metropolitan Life Insurance Company

MALE

IDEAL WEIGHT CHART

HEIGHT (with shoes)	SMALL FRAME	MEDIUM FRAME	LARGE FRAME
5 ft. 2 in.	112-120	118-129	126-141
5 ft. 3 in.	115-123	121-133	129-144
5 ft. 4 in.	118-126	124-136	132-148
5 ft. 5 in.	121-129	127-139	135-152
5 ft. 6 in.	124-133	130-143	138-156
5 ft. 7 in.	128-137	134-147	142-161
5 ft. 8 in.	132-141	138-152	147-166
5 ft. 9 in.	136-145	142-156	151-170

38 / *Candy, Chocolate, Ice Cream and How to Lick 'em!*

5 ft. 10 in.	140-150	146-160	155-174
5 ft. 11 in.	144-154	150-165	159-179
6 ft. 0 in.	148-158	154-170	164-184
6 ft. 1 in.	152-162	158-175	168-189
6 ft. 2 in.	156-167	162-180	173-194
6 ft. 3 in.	160-171	167-185	178-199
6 ft. 4 in.	164-175	172-190	182-204

SHOWS MINIMUM TO MAXIMUM WEIGHTS
Courtesy, Metropolitan Life Insurance Company

YOUR *On Diet* DAY CALORIE QUOTA. *Plan your On Diet day allotment at no more than 900 calories, no matter how much you weigh, how tall you are, whatever your age, and whatever your activities are,* provided your doctor approves, of course.

Whenever I would go to a health spa or to a private physician for a diet, I would invariably be put on 900 calories per day. This is considered by experts to be a safe, nutritional daily minimum. If you have any question regarding what *your* safe daily minimum should be, check with your physician.

Many days I even ate less than 900 calories. Naturally, the less I ate, the more I lost!

YOUR *Off Diet* DAY CALORIE QUOTA. Use the chart opposite to determine the number of calories for your *Off Diet* days: use either the section for men or women, find your Ideal Weight, then read across to your age group to determine your calorie intake for your *Off Diet* day.

IDEAL WEIGHT	CALORIE ALLOWANCE		
Pounds	25 Years	45 Years	65 Years
MEN			
110	2,300	2,050	1,750
121	2,450	2,200	1,850
132	2,600	2,350	1,950
143	2,750	2,500	2,100
154	2,900	2,600	2,200
165	3,050	2,750	2,300
176	3,200	2,900	2,450
187	3,350	3,050	2,550
WOMEN			
88	1,600	1,450	1,200
99	1,750	1,600	1,300
110	1,900	1,700	1,450
121	2,000	1,800	1,550
128	2,100	1,900	1,600
132	2,150	1,950	1,650
143	2,300	2,050	1,750
154	2,400	2,200	1,850

Courtesy of The Nutrition Board of The National Academy of Sciences

PERSONAL ADJUSTMENTS. Naturally, no chart can provide exact information for your particular body; therefore, expect to make slight adjustments as you go along. For example, you will note that the above chart shows caloric differences for different age groups. Many books on nutrition indicate that as people mature their metabolisms slow down and they require less food. They also specify if you are a particularly nervous or active person or if you do heavy work, increase the caloric amount given for your age group by 10 percent. On the other hand, if you are sedentary, decrease the figure by 10 percent. For example, if your Ideal Weight is 120 and you are a normally active forty-five year-old woman, consume 1,800 on your *Off Diet* days. If, however, you are extremely active, consume 1,980 calories per *Off Diet* day. If you are sedentary, consume up to 1,620 calories on your *Off Diet* day.

HOW MUCH WILL YOU LOSE AND HOW QUICKLY WILL YOU LOSE IT? You can lose as much as you want on any diet, *if you can stick to it long enough.* Fads and crash diets show spectacular weight losses in a very short period, but they are too restrictive to stay on for more than a few weeks at the most. Recidivism is immediate and inevitable. (Don't we know it!)

On the contrary, the *On/Off Diet* is well-balanced. *It satisfies the nutritional requirements that the body needs while it allows the indulgences that the emotions crave.*

Some of those who have been trying the *On/Off Diet* have lost 5 pounds the first week and 2 to 3 pounds every week thereafter. Others have lost a pound a week. But 1 pound a week is 52 pounds a year and half of that time you are enjoying *Off Diet* days!

Serious dieting is a declaration of war! Prepare for doing battle! Be certain you have all of the necessary fat-fighting equipment:

A CALORIE COUNTER. Checking calories is a drag! It's like exercising. It's not much fun but it certainly pays off in the long run. And like exercising, it gets easier and more worthwhile the longer you do it. It won't be long before you will remember the caloric value of the foods you eat regularly and you will not have to refer to the counter as often. It is similar to traveling a strange road and needing to refer to a map. Each time you take the same trip, the route becomes more familiar and you rely on the map less often.

I used to stay up nights eating. Now I stay up reading to find out caloric values of as many different foods as possible! The more you familiarize yourself with calories, the more varied and interesting your daily menus will become and thus it will be more pleasurable to reach and stay at your Ideal Weight.

The *Candy, Chocolate, Ice Cream and How to Count 'em* Calorie Counter at the back of the book beginning on page 107 was compiled specially for the *obesie* with a taste for fun foods and a mind toward good health. In addition to hundreds of listings of foods *obesies* crave, we have included natural and organic foods never before gathered between two covers. (A neophyte dieter pointed out that none of the other calorie counters he has read includes the caloric value of water. We have it listed under "Beverages." You can drink as much water as you want—it has no calories. You may even bathe in it, if you wish!)

There is a grouping on "Prepared Foods," such as TV dinners, to help you compute short-order thawing and heating at home.

For those evenings when you are dining out, the *Candy, Chocolate, Ice Cream and How to Count'em* Calorie Counter has a special section devoted to typical fare of different popular cuisines: Chinese, Italian, etc.

This calorie counter is probably the "safest" and easiest-to-use of all counters on the market because we have rounded out the figure of each item to the next highest five; for example, 33 calories became 35; 37 became 40. Your recorded total for the day will undoubtedly be a little higher than the actual number of calories you have consumed. We did this deliberately to provide a safety valve in the event you have inadvertently miscalculated your caloric intake. This could occur if the piece of meat you're eating isn't as lean as the meat analyzed in the counter or if the apple you're about to bite into is a bit larger than the one listed.

Rounding out the calories makes it easier for you to keep a tally of your daily caloric intake. It's always best to write down the calories of meals as you eat them, but if you must keep a mental running account because you are also on the run, the rounded out figures make your task much easier.

A SMALL FOOD SCALE AND A MEASURING CUP to determine volume and/or weight. When calculating calories it is essential to know the kind of measurements used. *Fluid* ounces is a measure of volume or capacity (how much space something occupies). To determine volume always use a *measuring cup*. *Net* ounces refers to the weight of an item and is determined by using a *scale*. All packaging specifies either *Fluid* ounces or *Net* ounces and you should read carefully before measuring. In the calorie counter when the measurement "cup" is indicated, you should use a measuring cup. When ounces are given, a small food scale should be used.

A POCKET DIARY. Buy a small pocket diary to record the number of calories you consume each day and your weight each week. Mark each day of the month with your daily calorie quota. Then you will have no excuse for forgetting whether it is an *On Diet* day or an *Off Diet* day.

A BATHROOM SCALE. When dieting have your Calorie Counter at your fingertips and a scale at your toes.

For centuries people have been pondering Mona Lisa's enigmatic smile. If Leonardo da Vinci had painted a full length portrait of her we would see that she's standing on her bathroom scale, beaming because she's just discovered she has reached her Ideal Weight on the *On/Off Diet!* If you have stuck to your diet nothing is a greater source of joy than your scale.

Your weight will vary from scale to scale. Therefore, it is important to *use the same scale every time you weigh yourself.*

When I was on the *On/Off Diet* I weighed myself every day since it was part of the "scientific experiment" I was conducting, but checking your weight every day may be discouraging, particularly on this diet. Your weight might go up very slightly after an *Off Diet* day. If the weight does not drop the very next day (it may be that time of the month or your body may not have eliminated wastes efficiently) you may become alarmed and think the diet is not working. *Weight loss is a cumulative happening.* As much as three and a half pounds in one week may not manifest itself as a half a pound every day. Even if it did, a half pound would not always register on some scales. Therefore, *weigh in about once a week, after an On Diet day,* preferably before breakfast or at the same hour each time you weigh. (Once you have reached your Ideal Weight and are maintaining it, you must weigh yourself every day—but more about this later on.)

So now you have determined your Ideal Weight, the goal you wish to reach.

And you have determined your Caloric Quota for your *Off Diet* day. You understand you can have no more than 900 calories on your *On Diet* day.

You have your calorie counter, food scale, measuring cup,

pocket diary, and bathroom scale at the ready, poised for action.

Further on in the book are menus to help you plan meals for *On* and *Off Diet* days.

All you need now is a little *won't power*. Anyone can say, "I *will* eat it." The trick is to say, "I won't!" IF YOUR WILL POWER WON'T WORK, MAYBE YOUR WON'T POWER WILL!

Now is the time to try it!

8

On the *On/Off Diet*

Welcome aboard the *On /Off Diet*, your own personal flight from fat. Fasten your safety belts (you'll be pulling them in more and more) and prepare for taking off—all that excess baggage!

Once you have determined from your doctor that you are able to diet, check to see if you have a special occasion in the near future. If you do, consider that day an *Off Diet* day. Now count back to today (or the day you want to start) to see if it is an *On Diet* day or an *Off Diet* eay.

If you have decided that tomorrow is *the* day to start, what do you do today? Stuff yourself silly waiting for the dawn? Don't! You will probably put on five pounds and set yourself back two weeks.

TIPS EN ROUTE. The following are guidelines and hints to make your trip more successful and pleasant:

CALORIES CANNOT BE SAVED FROM ONE DAY TO THE NEXT. Suppose on one 2,000 calorie day you ate only 1,600 calories. May you add the unused 400 calories to the following day's allotment? Absolutely not! *You are trying to acclimate your body to eating the number of calories it needs to maintain your Ideal Weight* which is 2,000 calories, not 1,600. Nor can you carry uneaten calories over from your 900 calorie day. Once the day is gone, so are its calories!

PLAN AHEAD. Each morning think about the distribution of your caloric allotment. Compute your calories ahead for the entire day. Meeting a friend for lunch? Then think about the menu beforehand and check out the calories of a few special dishes you are certain will be on the bill of fare. When I am invited to a sumptious, scrumptious lunch which I know will run close to my entire daily quota, I have a glass of water for breakfast and a stick of Trident for dinner!

If you generally consume most of your day's calories in the evenings, you don't have to change your way of living because you're dieting. Just be certain to save up your calories so that you have them in reserve for when you feel you really "need" them.

When planning meals at home, learn to budget your calories as you do your money. Bargain hunt to find foods that are filling, nutritious, tasty and low in calories.

Refer to your pocket diary whenever you are making social engagements. Entertain on an *Off Diet* day to make *On Diet* days as easy as possible. If you must dine out on an *On Diet* day, choose a restaurant that can prepare food exactly as you require it: broiled fish without butter, salad with lemon only for dressing, etc. Stay away from snack bars and fast food restaurants on your *On Diet* days. They are usually very low on low calorie food. *On Diet* days on the job, bring your lunch with you rather than be tempted by the devil's food.

STOP, LOOK, AND CHEW! Make meal-time a special-time, even when alone. Set a pretty table, prepare food attractively, light candles, put on your favorite music and relax. *Relish and savor each bite.* Eating should be an occasion. Dine, don't devour!

NIBBLING. It's easy for non-*obesies* to tell us *obesies* not to nibble. We nibble to relieve nervous tension and if we couldn't nibble we would go up the wall! But nibbles and slivers and smidgeons are almost impossible to compute calorically. If they are high-calorie-nibbles, they can send our daily intake well above our quota. Moreover, indiscriminate nibbling leads to binging! Therefore, for *On Diet* days or emotionally difficult *Off Diet* days, anticipate anxiety attacks by preparing low-calorie-nibbles.

A "raw vegetable nibble bowl" to be eaten with the fingers to take the place of chips, nuts, or candy might include: cut up celery, cauliflower, cucumbers, lettuce, raw mushrooms, red and green peppers, radishes, cabbage, and spinach.

Low-calorie dishes that are great for late night snacking are:
- Tomatoes grilled with a light sprinkling of Parmesan cheese and oregano.
- Chopped raw tomatoes, raw onions, cooked asparagus, cooked string beans, cooked carrots, pimentos, all of which have been marinated overnight in vinegar or your favorite low-calorie dressing. To be eaten cold. (Some people like to include cut-up hot peppers for tang. Spicy food, however, activates my taste buds and increases my appetite. Therefore, I use hot ingredients sparingly.)
- Tiny, boiled shrimp, dabbed, not doused, in cocktail

sauce. Each shrimp to be eaten individually with a toothpick. (It takes longer that way!)
- Blueberries eaten individually with a toothpick.

Compute the calories of the *entire* dish as you prepare it. (You can estimate the calories of a whole cucumber much more easily than you can one slice.) Then you can feel free to nibble away without worrying about counting each mouthful you take.

On the *Mame* tour I started knitting and crocheting which help relieve nervous tension for me. I discovered that if I keep my hands moving while I'm watching television or waiting to go on stage, it's easier to keep my mouth still! Why don't you start knitting, crocheting, or doing needlepoint instead of nibbling? The wool is a bitch to digest, but that's what makes it so non-fattening!

"SMOKING, DRINKING, NEVER THINKING OF TOMORROW." Alcohol, which has calories, and marijuana, which has none, both diminish will power. Studies show that marijuana, particularly, stimulates appetite. I suggest you abstain from both on *On Diet* days.

HITTING A PLATEAU. If at some time your weight refuses to budge, in spite of all your conscientious effort, your body may merely be replacing the disappearing fat by retaining water.

When you hit a plateau, hang on! *Kick the scale, but stick to the diet.* You will see that after a week or even a few days the excess water causing the problem will be voided and your scale will leap to a new low!

I hit a plateau on the *On/Off Diet* when I was but a few pounds away from my Ideal Weight. It was a snowy, bleak,

STOP, LOOK, AND CHEW! Make meal-time a special-time, even when alone. Set a pretty table, prepare food attractively, light candles, put on your favorite music and relax. *Relish and savor each bite.* Eating should be an occasion. Dine, don't devour!

NIBBLING. It's easy for non-*obesies* to tell us *obesies* not to nibble. We nibble to relieve nervous tension and if we couldn't nibble we would go up the wall! But nibbles and slivers and smidgeons are almost impossible to compute calorically. If they are high-calorie-nibbles, they can send our daily intake well above our quota. Moreover, indiscriminate nibbling leads to binging! Therefore, for On Diet days or emotionally difficult Off Diet days, anticipate anxiety attacks by preparing low-calorie-nibbles.

A "raw vegetable nibble bowl" to be eaten with the fingers to take the place of chips, nuts, or candy might include: cut up celery, cauliflower, cucumbers, lettuce, raw mushrooms, red and green peppers, radishes, cabbage, and spinach.

Low-calorie dishes that are great for late night snacking are:
- Tomatoes grilled with a light sprinkling of Parmesan cheese and oregano.
- Chopped raw tomatoes, raw onions, cooked asparagus, cooked string beans, cooked carrots, pimentos, all of which have been marinated overnight in vinegar or your favorite low-calorie dressing. To be eaten cold. (Some people like to include cut-up hot peppers for tang. Spicy food, however, activates my taste buds and increases my appetite. Therefore, I use hot ingredients sparingly.)
- Tiny, boiled shrimp, dabbed, not doused, in cocktail

sauce. Each shrimp to be eaten individually with a toothpick. (It takes longer that way!)
- Blueberries eaten individually with a toothpick.

Compute the calories of the *entire* dish as you prepare it. (You can estimate the calories of a whole cucumber much more easily than you can one slice.) Then you can feel free to nibble away without worrying about counting each mouthful you take.

On the *Mame* tour I started knitting and crocheting which help relieve nervous tension for me. I discovered that if I keep my hands moving while I'm watching television or waiting to go on stage, it's easier to keep my mouth still! Why don't you start knitting, crocheting, or doing needlepoint instead of nibbling? The wool is a bitch to digest, but that's what makes it so non-fattening!

"SMOKING, DRINKING, NEVER THINKING OF TOMORROW." Alcohol, which has calories, and marijuana, which has none, both diminish will power. Studies show that marijuana, particularly, stimulates appetite. I suggest you abstain from both on *On Diet* days.

HITTING A PLATEAU. If at some time your weight refuses to budge, in spite of all your conscientious effort, your body may merely be replacing the disappearing fat by retaining water.

When you hit a plateau, hang on! *Kick the scale, but stick to the diet.* You will see that after a week or even a few days the excess water causing the problem will be voided and your scale will leap to a new low!

I hit a plateau on the *On/Off Diet* when I was but a few pounds away from my Ideal Weight. It was a snowy, bleak,

February morning in Dodge City, Kansas. I was so disgusted I almost cried. I didn't want to step on my scale. For the past seven torturous mornings that unblinking monster had stubbornly, defiantly, contemptuously frozen at 143.

Was Dodge City the end of the trail?

Finally, I creaked out of my bed and onto my scale. I looked down in pure hate at the devil's tine below me. I stared in total disbelief. *141!* I had lost two pounds overnight and dropped off my plateau into what seemed like Paradise—one pound away from my Ideal Weight!

NOTHING IS FATTENING! No food is *fattening* on the *On/Off Diet*. No matter how many calories, it only adds weight if the *quantity* you eat catapults you over your daily quota. Even grapefruit is *fattening* if you eat it when you have no more calories left. But a piece of coconut custard cream pie is not *fattening* if you have its calories to spend.

Eating a mere 100 calories (as in one ounce of cheese) more than your body can burn up will add 10 additional pounds in one year. Think about that when you are finishing the leftovers from Junior's lunch because you don't want them to go to waste. If it doesn't go to waste, it will go to waist!

SURVIVAL KIT. Prepare a survival kit for *On Diet* days. Keep a fork, knife, spoon, straws, artificial sweeteners, low-calorie crackers, sugarless gum, and protein tablets in a plastic bag and tuck it into your purse or briefcase. During the day pop into any grocery store and buy plain yogurt, diet soda, fresh fruit, cottage cheese and snack on them. I keep cinnamon and low-calorie jams in my survival kit to perk up plain cottage cheese. A teaspoon or two of low-calorie jam sweetens and flavors plain yogurt without adding many additional calories.

(One container of plain yogurt and two tablespoonsful of diet strawberry jam are only 136 calories. A container of regular strawberry yogurt can be as high as 270 calories.)

There are many times when survival kits will save calories: in an office to combat the cake that comes with coffee breaks; in the glove compartment of your car to fight temptation when the family wants to eat at a drive-in.

If you travel, pack your survival kit in your attaché case or tote bag and keep it within easy reach aboard a plane or train.

Slim Shakes. Also included in my survival kit are the ingredients for a coffee or cocoa Slim Shake. What's a Slim Shake? It's a great drink for On Diet days when you need something low calorie and filling. It's a great drink for Off Diet days when you want something frothy and refreshing without the calories of a regular shake.

I keep three teaspoons of non-fat dry milk and one teaspoon of instant coffee or a half teaspoon unsweetened cocoa in a plastic packet in my kit. (The recipe for the basic Slim Shake and variations that can be made at home are in the Menu and Recipe chapter on page 88.)

I go into any soda fountain and ask them to mix the ingredients with a cup of crushed ice, a half cup of water, and artificial sweetner in their malted machine.

I've asked countermen across the country to prepare Slim Shakes for me and I have never been refused. Recently . . . it was 4:00 p.m. on a hot Texas afternoon and we had just finished our first day of rehearsal for *Last of the Red Hot Lovers*. I was hungry but it was much too early to start thinking about dinner, so I took my Slim Shake packet to a local soda fountain. The man sitting next to me overheard my instructions and was curious.

"What's a Slim Shake, ma'am?"

When I told him it was a delicious 42 calorie milkshake he asked "How can anything be delicious and have only 42 calories?" When the drink was served I asked him to taste it. He immediately wheeled around to the woman sitting next to him and said, "Ethel, dammit, this is what *you* should be having!"

The counterman approached with a spoon in hand, "I have a wife at home... a little round... and I'd like to tell her about it." He tasted it and beamed. Then a real-live Texas cowboy—ten gallon hat, dusty boots, faded jeans—leaned over in curiosity. "Try it, you'll like it!" I told him. Well, I don't believe he ate the whole thing!

When I started to leave, Ethel turned from her 442 calorie malted milkshake, peered over her very well-rounded shoulder, stared at me for a moment and said, "Well, Harold, she's certainly not *that* slim!"

Audrey Hepburn I'm not, but I am slimmer than I have ever been in my adult life. If you drink Slim Shakes instead of high calorie filler-uppers you probably will be too!

LIVE IT UP... A LOT! Those of us for whom food was a primary source of entertainment and yes, even excitement, must consciously seek other areas of activities. Having a good time socially does not necessarily mean going out to dinner or eating every hors d'oeuvre on the buffet. Meet a friend and see a show, attend a concert, visit a museum. Staying at home? There's fun there too. Sewing, painting, woodworking, playing an instrument can all be relaxing. Get into bed early with a good book, or better still with a great mate! Believe me, when dieting, copulation helps you cope! That's an old Anglo-Saxon method of weight loss that worked wonders then and still does!

I practiced the *On/Off Diet* strictly for one month before I could actually say that I felt it had become a habit. Some friends were in the swing in three weeks, others in six. The time varies. Adhere to your *On/Off Diet* without deviating for at least five weeks. Do not exchange *On Diet* days for *Off Diet* days during that five week training period. After five weeks you may replace an *On Diet* day for an *Off Diet* day for a very special occasion (such as the advent of Halley's Comet). Schedule two *On Diet* days in a row in order to have an *Off Diet* day coincide with a special occasion.

Do not play switch every week! If you have a regular Thursday luncheon and Friday bridge game, be happy that on this program you can at least eat-it-up with *one* of the groups every week! Do not plan two *Off Diet* days in a row until you have reached your Ideal Weight.

The *On/Off Diet* can be the greatest trip of them all because "getting there is half the fun!" Count your calories carefully, don't exceed your daily quotas, follow the tips, and you'll make a beautiful landing at your Ideal Weight—probably well ahead of your estimated time of arrival. Best of all, *you*'ll be the sight worth seeing!

9

A Brand New Habit

"You'll never be slim until you learn to eat *sensibly*. You must change your eating habits!"

How many times have we heard it? How many times have we read it? How many books, programs, well-meaning friends and relatives suggest diets so low in calories that even if we would stick with them, they have no insight into the needs of our bodies or the passions of our palates. What person who requires 2,000 calories per day would form a *lasting* habit by consuming 750 calories per day? How *sensible* is that?

The *On/Off Diet* offers a double whammy: *you lose weight and at the same time you train yourself to eat sensibly and maintain your Ideal Weight!*

I used to think that when a diet was over I could eat as much as I wanted. I've learned now that I can't. Nobody can! I now stop eating when I've consumed 2,000 calories because that's what I've been *reconditioned* to do by the *On/Off Diet*. Now I have either salad dressing *or* soup *or* dessert, not all of them at one meal. The diet made me consider the caloric value of food *before* I ate it: Is a sugar wafer worth 50 calories or wouldn't a tangerine be more satisfying? Shouldn't I have broiled fish rather than steak so I can enjoy the special dessert offered?

The diet also helped make a habit of moderation and moderation is a must for the *obesie*, who unlike the addict and the alcoholic, cannot give up his drug entirely. But in the *obesie*, nature's built-in-mechanism faltered because it had been tampered with in many different and sometimes subtle ways. We need to get those mechanisms working again, but just as there are very few overnight sensations in the theater, or anywhere else for that matter, it takes time to develop self-awareness to form new habits. During this training period, the On/Off Diet works as an understudy to an *obesie*'s ailing appestat and absent will power. The On/Off Diet provides the yardstick which enables the *obesie* to eat all available food in moderate quantities. Now I can sense when I've reached my daily calorie quota. I don't have to keep as careful a running account as I did when I first started the diet.

At one time I joined Weight Watchers which promised weight reduction and a complete re-education of my eating habits in sixteen weeks. I stuck to their diet fanatically. I went to "confession" each week and I lost 22 pounds in the prescribed period. When I received my graduation pin with the stone which signified I had lost over 20 pounds, it seemed as though that stone had been produced by the gall of my own denial. I headed for the refrigerator and didn't come out for the next sixteen weeks during which I gained 32 pounds.

Why?

I had been deprived of practically every eating pleasure during those sixteen weeks. I was dying for a *lick* of ice cream, a *crumb* of cake, a *sip* of martini, a *grain* of rice, a *kernel* of corn, even an olive *pit*! The joy of special occasions was diluted. What do you stuff a Thanksgiving turkey with —your fist? Can you toast a bride and groom with sauerkraut juice? Blahh! Even Saturdays at the movies was ruined: have you ever gone to a theater where they sold hot salted cauliflower?

I've even run from 0 to 60 grams on various low carbohydrate diets. They permitted me an *occasional* scotch—but I'm a very sociable woman and there are many occasions! And what about parties? Do I put candles on a birthday *steak*!

Eating is part of the sensuality of life. Good food is part of good living and if you really enjoy living you really enjoy food. When you eat a deliciously, delectable, high calorie delight, you're not being bad, you're being human. Robots don't dig food. People do! Patrice Munsel once said, "I never really trust anyone who doesn't like to eat." She's absolutely right!

But there is a big difference between enjoying food and being engulfed by it. The *On/Off Diet* helps *obesies* convert compulsive craving into controlled enjoyment.

There is a Silent Majority of the many weight-loss programs existing in America today: those who invariably return to fat because their diets have not trained them to *maintain* their weight loss. These recidivists never speak of weight *regained*. They never publicly count calories while *binging*. They never boast about buying a size *larger* garment. They never show off newly acquired *fat* figures. They keep grocers stocking diet foods, health spas opening new branches, and doctors prescribing more diet pills. There are over 100 million weight-regainers in the United States alone. A huge figure, in every way, but only a part of the 78 percent of all Americans who are overweight!

I realize that in a democracy it's usually advantageous to be part of the majority but now that, thanks to the *On/Off Diet*, I am able to maintain my Ideal Weight, I have become one of a minority group, the "Slim Elite" and I prefer it. Prefer it? I love it and so will you!

10

Off the *On/Off Diet*

You've reached your destination! You're at your Ideal Weight! Well, hello, gorgeous! Yes, that's really *your* weight on the scale. Yes, that's really *you* in the mirror, a sylph of your former fat self!

As you look in that mirror the question not to ask is, "Who is the fairest of them all?" That's apparent—it's you! Ask instead, *"It's off, but for how long?"*

I don't mean to sound like the wicked old witch, but how much weight have you lost and then regained over and over and over again? If I added it all up my total would be *close to a thousand pounds*.

Look in the mirror, but a different mirror, the mirror of your mind, to increase your awareness of your loss-gain-loss-gain syndrome.

Compulsive eating is incurable, but it is controllable. Obesity will ever smolder, ready to flare into fat whenever you are particularly vulnerable:

- When your friends all seem to disappear in a puff of pique.
- When your boss screams at you and he's wrong.

- When your wife screams at you and she's right.
- When no one's handing you a line—of credit—anymore.
- When you can't make it.
- When you can make it but there's no one there to make it with!

Whatever you do at these times, don't open the flood-gates and let the food pour in! Don't rationalize your way to the refrigerator! Don't add inches to injury! This time you have help from your friends, the *On/Off Diet* and your insight into your vulnerabilities!

Because you no longer need to lose weight does not mean that you no longer need to be introspective. As you questioned yourself each time you had the need to overeat while you were on the *On/Off Diet* you must continue to do so now. Feel a binge coming on? Wheel out the "won't power" by asking yourself what it is you *really* want!

The reasons why someone had been fat do not just melt away as the fat disappears. All the occurrences of my life which had contributed to my being an *obesie* in the first place, *still are happening to me.* Many of the ways in which I used fat and food (as mentioned in Chapter 4) are *still* operative today, but to a much lesser degree. That is why this moment of thin could also be the time of terror. We cling to old ways because they are so much more familiar and "comfortable," even if they are unhealthy. That is why the post-diet period is the most difficult.

Some *obesies* will unconsciously resist giving up their overweight because they have used it as a defensive weapon. They flaunt fat in much the way others thumb their noses or "raspberry." Once thin, they feel lost without that means to vent their feelings.

Other *obesies* use their fat as a protective shield to help them hide from normal problems. They have literally put up a wall between themselves and the world which, when gone, leaves the *obesie* seemingly defenseless. That is why so many of us rebuild that wall pound by awful pound.

Thinness means peeling off: peeling off weight, peeling off inhibitions, exposing more of your essential self to the world. Shrinking your stomach will expand your horizons. When you are more attractive physically, more demands will be made of you to participate in life: socially, in business, and in bed! Those demands can be so frightening that some *obesies* can't cope and they regain weight to put themselves in hiding again.

The size of the roles I played changed in inverse proportion to my weight. As I weighed less and less I was considered for larger and larger parts. I am now faced with greater responsibilities in my work, but at the same time the rewards are so much greater than they were when I was doing only character bits.

NOW IS THE TIME TO BE MORE INTROSPECTIVE THAN EVER!

STEPPING OFF THE DIET. *Because you no longer have to lose weight does not mean that you are now able to lose control! You will still be counting calories. You still must be aware of the number of calories you eat each day.* Most thin people don't call being conscious of calories "dieting." They consider it a way of life and so must you.

As an actress I have a portfolio which I carry with me when I make "rounds" of the offices of agents and producers. Invariably, someone will compare the photographs which were taken of me before I started the *On/Off Diet* with those of me now. (The first comment is how much *younger* I look in the more *recent* pictures. It's true! Each 15 pounds off my weight seemed to take five years off my age!) Whenever they are referred to as "Before" and "After" shots, I'm quick to explain that they are "Before" and "During," that there is never an "after-diet-time." I must always be conscious of the number of calories I consume every day. I must always be aware that I am "allergic" to food. Too much of it causes me to break out in huge welts—fat!

Now your daily calorie quota will be the same every day. Begin to eliminate your *On Diet* days *gradually*, now that you have reached your Ideal Weight. Cut out one *On Diet* day the first week, another *On Diet* day the second week, another *On Diet* day the third week, until in four weeks you have eliminated *On Diet* days completely. If during this gradual tapering off period of *On Diet* days you discover that you are gaining weight, reduce your *Off Diet* day calorie quota by 10 percent to compensate for no longer having as many *On Diet*-900 calorie days. For example, if your *Off Diet* day quota is 2,100 you may have to decrease it to 2,000. I had to make this adjustment. Or the opposite might be true. You might continue to lose weight after eliminating all the *On Diet* days. In that case, *increase* your caloric intake by 10 percent in order to maintain your Ideal Weight.

SETTING A NEW IDEAL WEIGHT. Perhaps the Ideal Weight you had set for yourself is not as low as you wish it to be. You now want to lose a few more pounds. Decide on your new Ideal Weight, recheck the chart on page 37 to determine the number of calories needed to maintain this new weight, set that amount as your new *Off Diet* day quota. Then, continue the *On/Off Diet* until your new Ideal Weight has been reached.

A WEIGH A DAY. You had been weighing yourself only once a week during the *On/Off Diet.* Now begin weighing yourself every morning. Your scale should become as much a part of your morning toilette as your toothbrush. Mirrors don't show subtle pound changes, scales do!

SLIPPAGE. My own slippage occurs almost bite by bite. Gradually it could work its way into a whopper of a binge if I were not careful. (No fun, you say, being careful all the time. *It's much more fun than being fat! Remember how you used to HATE YOURSELF?*) Accelerated eating is another hallmark of the *obesie* personality that could set our overweight zooming from zero to 60 in seemingly less than a minute. That rate of increase may be fine for race cars, but it's definitely off the track for us!

If you notice even a slight rise in your weight, check yourself that very day by computing the number of calories in the food you ate. Although you think you know the value of each item, refer to your calorie counter to make absolutely certain that you have not misvalued or miscalculated. Perhaps you had a four ounce hamburger and counted it as three ounces. Are the wine glasses in most restaurants a little larger than the one you usually use at home? Are you beginning to order an appetizer in addition to the salad dressing or dessert? Do you now have a pat of butter or two in the baked potato? A double scoop cone instead of a single? A small error, omission, or change in eating pattern day after day after day could throw your figures and your figure off tremendously!

DON'T WEAKEN ON WEEKENDS! DON'T GO OVER YOUR DAILY CALORIE QUOTA ON VACATIONS! I know, you say you will diet during the week or when your vacation is over, but it is dangerous from two standpoints: first, each weekend you will be getting out of the *habit* of eating the number of calories that *maintain* your sensational shape. Second, it precludes enjoying yourself at weekday celebrations, cocktail parties after work, a dinner date after Thursday night shopping; an irresistible cake at Friday's bridge game. If you stay within your daily quota *every* day, you will never have to deprive yourself of anything on any day! Remember the weekend is only two days long, while the week is *five*!

We *obesies* have to be especially careful on vacation. A cruise doesn't have to be a giant floating meal where you go off the deep end! Don't let American Plan resorts let you smash your newly acquired figure against their dining room table because what you eat is included in the cost of your room. For that matter, tennis, shuffleboard, volleyball and badminton courts, the swimming pools, pingpong tables, and boating facilities are all part of the plan.

The morning after you return from a trip, *weigh in*. Remember, a pound gained Sunday is easier to take off Monday before it doubles itself by Tuesday, establishes squatters rights on Wednesday, and becomes part of the territory by Thursday. But if you try to *crash diet* newly acquired pounds off, you will be starving on the second day, desperate on the third, and gorging on the fourth. Don't undo the glorious habit that started your success. Do go right back on the *On/Off Diet!* If you keep the habit up, the habit will keep you down!

I was determined to stay at my Ideal Weight when the *Mame* touring company arrived in New Orleans four days before Easter. I had been in a beautiful holding pattern at 140 for six weeks during which I had been slowly eliminating my On Diet days and substituting Off Diet days.

Now in New Orleans, a city noted for its incomparable

French cuisine and all that jazz, I was off the diet completely and here my new habit would be given its greatest stress test. If I could get through four glorious days and four glorious nights—twelve glorious meals—without gaining weight here, I knew I could make it anywhere in the world.

I was particularly concerned because I remember only too well what had happened on my first trip to New Orleans several years before with "Mrs. America." The city was at "Mrs. America's" feet and I was at my fork! In that four day visit I gained 12 pounds. Unbelieveable but true!

Now years later I was back, slim, and I had resolved to remain slim. But I wanted to enjoy the food and the same places I had been to before. And did I! On our day off, this is what I had:

Breakfast

Two pillows and a snooze—I slept until noon!

Brunch at Brennan's

Eggs Bonnet Carré	
Each forkful must have contained 100 calories. I stopped at five.	500
House muffin	135
With 1 T. Strawberry preserves	50
Flaming Bananas Foster (I bet Mrs. Foster never served anything like *that* to Stephen in their Old Kentucky Home.) Each bite was certainly 200 calories. I had two.	400
Brandy, compliments of the Maitre d'	75

While roaming the French Quarter

1 Scotch	100
6 huge raw oysters from a marbled counter stand that served them straight from the nets they were caught in	100
with sauce	50
½ of a Praline (I shipped the rest of the box home!)	150

At the Sazarac Room of the Roosevelt Hotel

1 Ramos Gin Fizz	150

Swinging with the Jazz at Presentation Hall

Great sound	0

Toasting the dawn at The Cafe Du Monde

Hot donut—three were on the plate, I settled for one!	150
Steaming chicory coffee, black	0
TOTAL	1860

The total of all these rich epicurean delights was only 1,860 calories. Because I had not gone crazy, a taste had become more thrilling than a ton!

I went to bed thinking of a remark by Pierette, the sister of the well-known gastronomic writer, Brillat-Savarin, who expired at table shortly before her hundredth birthday: "Bring on the dessert, I think I'm about to die!"

I would have died happily that night for I had received *my* just desserts: I had successfully and permanently made the metamorphosis from glutton to gourmet!

11

Freud and Food

Sigmund Freud, the great mastermind of mastering the mind, said, *"The most powerful urge is to seek pleasure and avoid pain."* This made me understand why whenever I had experienced the psychological and/or physical pain of a diet—the pain of denial—I had to replace it as soon as possible with the pleasure of food. An *obesie*'s pain is at least doubled when he diets. He has to deal with his usual, everyday anxiety which made him overeat in the first place, plus he has to deal with the added tension and physical discomfort of dieting. His pain is increased in inverse proportion to his pleasure.

Most diets require strong motivation to withstand this long-term denial. On the *On/Off Diet,* periods of denial are very short and they share *equal time* with periods of pleasure. Do you dig artichokes doused in butter? Then why choke on chicory? If you love rich Irish coffee why sip unsweetened Chinese tea! Could cottage cheese ever replace cheese fondue? The *On/Off Diet* well-balanced menus can be custom-made for the preferences of each and every palate and each and every life style. It permits you all the food you love in sensible quantities that will help you reach and maintain your Ideal Weight.

cheese cake in the world. I championed the Turf Restaurant in New York City, she extolled the Fairmont in Dallas. Months later after performing at the Fairmont, she returned to New York with "Exhibit A."

I was *delighted* to play judge and jury! I gladly awarded the decision in flavor of Miss Adams and the Fairmont. Part of the reason the Fairmont's tasted so incredibly good must have been that it was my very first piece of "no-guilt cheese cake."

As long as you stay within your daily calorie quota, gone is the pain of denial, gone is the pain of guilt. Now, thanks to the On/Off Diet, all the foods you've ever hungered for, dreamed of, drooled over, and longed for are yours for the eating. At last they will bring you only pleasure!

The *On/Off Diet* gave me 2,100 calories every other day and once I reached my Ideal Weight 2,000 calories *every* day. How would you feel if someone gave you $2,000? Wouldn't that give you pleasure? But suppose they told you exactly how you had to spend it? The *On/Off Diet* gives me the pleasure of spending my "fortune" as I wish. I'm not limited to all protein or all rice or all vegetables or all of any one thing.

Recently a friend flew into New York from Portland. We started out the evening in the Village with cocktails and dinner at Chumley's, then uptown for a second view of *Fiddler on the Roof*. Later it was over to First Avenue for club hopping and good sound. At one point Dave said, "Sandy, isn't there some club you would particularly like to go to?"

"The Flick," I answered without missing a beat.

"The Flick? But that's an ice cream parlor!"

"You bet it is! You have been downing your calories in liquor while I've been cooling it with club soda. I've been waiting for a lick at the Flick."

Because I had counted my calories carefully and was still way below my daily caloric quota, I could have the pleasure of a hot fudge sundae without another pain the obesie feels . . . the pain of guilt!

Before the *On/Off Diet*, when I wasn't crash dieting, the pleasures of food made me constantly experience the pain of *guilt*. Until the *On/Off Diet* I never really truly, fully, completely, entirely enjoyed a piece of cheese cake because I always felt so damned *guilty* eating it.

During the summer of our *Mame* tour, Edie Adams and I would both occasionally go on an all-protein diet. One night after the show over a snack of hard boiled eggs, cottage cheese, and black coffee, we were fantisizing about our favourite desserts. An animated discussion began about the greatest

12

Living It Up While Taking It Off

"Am I pooped! I've been up all night *dieting!*" Staying at home alone dieting is certainly no fun, especially when all your friends are out swinging. The *On/Off Diet* lets you live it up while taking it off.

Many diet programs suggest you wait until the diet is over before you go out and have fun. This implies that when you have lost all the weight you wish, you'll be able to go to any party or any restaurant and eat *whatever* you want without consequence. This is not so! You will always have to be calorie careful if you want to keep those pounds off. The *On/Off Diet* encourages you to go out on some of your *Off Diet* days and trains you to be careful eating out as well as eating in.

There are always giant questions facing us when we eat out: Is the fish broiled with butter? What makes that low calorie vegetable taste so fantastic? How much heavy cream is lurking in that dressing on the fresh fruit? Don't be afraid to question the waiter.

Check your calorie counter *before going out* to determine what calories are contained in the foods a particular restaurant usually offers. (I have said that before but it bears repeating.) The *Candy, Chocolate, Ice Cream and How to Count 'em* Calorie Counter has a special section on dining out, listing typical fare of popular cuisines. Try to be realistic when you estimate the size of the portions and don't forget to compute the calories in all of the extras: bread and butter; the mix in a drink; sauces and dressings; croutons; relishes; the sugar wafer served with the ice cream. When you do, you'll find there is no reason you can't dine out and slim down too!

WHEN DINING OUT PLAY "GO FISH"! There's no better place to diet while dining out than in a seafood restaurant. (My father has his own special seafood diet: you see food but you don't eat it!)

Don't allow yourself to be drawn to drawn butter or fish fries, however. All smoked and fried fish are much higher in calories than baked or broiled. On a diet, batter does not make it better. When ordering lobster try it with cocktail sauce which has half the calories of butter. Instead of drippy cole slaw order a big green salad, undressed. When it comes to chowder, make yours Manhattan: it's much lower in calories than New England.

According to an article in *The Ladies Home Journal* by Dr. Morton Glenn, there is about one half ounce more protein in a pound of flat fish (flounder or sole) than in one pound of choice beef (including ribs without bone). That same pound of beef has 2,000 calories while the same pound of fish has 400 calories!

WHAT HAVE YOU GOT AT STEAK? It may be your figure when eating out at a steak house. Steer away from the potato and double up on the salad. Always ask for dressing (preferably oil and vinegar) on the side and dab, don't deluge the greens. Order the smallest steak offered and cut away all the fat. Fish is a better "protein buy" for the calories, but if you just love, love steak, go to it, as long as you don't beef yourself up in the process.

A NEW SLANT ON DIETING—CHINESE FOOD. At a Chinese restaurant, to make it easier to stay within your daily calorie quota, instead of eating white rice which has very few nutrients and approximately 400 calories per cooked cup, order Chinese vegetables which are less than 25 calories per cup. The dry noodles that everyone nibbles on while waiting for service are also high (approximately 250 calories per cup). Sip tea instead and leave room and calories for your main dish. Here again, fish is a much better calorie bargain than beef. Sweet and sour dishes, sometimes as high as 1,000 calories per cup, can sour your good intentions to stay within your daily caloric quota. Spare ribs? Eat them sparingly. They're high on the hog and high in calories.

Want to take twice as long to eat half as much? Try using chopsticks instead of silverware!

For dessert, instead of pineapple (85 calories per half cup when packed in heavy syrup) or ice cream (260 calories per half cup), order a fortune cookie. Discard the cookie, savor the fortune. Confucius say "When you stay on your diet, friends enjoy seeing less of you—more often!"

"MAMA MIA, THAT'S A SPICY MEAT BALL." If you stay within your daily calorie quota you *can* have a ball—or two at your favorite Italian restaurant. Antipasto with only a few drops of olive oil, fenucchi, eggplant, clams arreganata are lower calorie Italian fare. If I must have noodles with their oodles of calories, I resist the garlic bread and dessert and eat no more than half the pasta on my plate. Then I'm never afraid of going pasta point of no return!

PARTIES ARE FOR DIETERS TOO. You can have an "outasight" time as long as you don't eat yourself blind.

Ask the bartender to pour your liquor into a one ounce shot glass so you can measure your drink. In general, straight "hard" liquors are 100 calories per ounce. Dry wines are 95 calories per four ounces. Beer is 125 calories per eight ounces. Brandy is 75 calories per ounce. Champagne, 175 for six ounces. Bubbles have calories, too! And so do mixes! For a more detailed listing of calories in alcoholic beverages, refer to page 111 of the Calorie Counter.

One reason not to drink at all is that it reduces "won't power." The more you drink the harder it will be to resist other calorie-laden offerings, so when I attend many cocktail parties I order:

- *A Virgin Mary*. (It may be hard to find—virgins are scarce these days!) A Bloody Mary with all the spices but without vodka!
- *A Very Wet Martini*. Much dry Vermouth with a drop or two of gin.
- *A Scale Driver*. Orange juice *without* vodka. Sure to help point the needle of your scale in the right direction!
- *A Slim Pickin's*. Club soda with a slice of fresh lime.
- *Water and Scotch*. A tall glass with ice, water, and a *splash* of scotch.
- *A Calf Shot*. A Bull Shot (spiced up bouillon and vodka) *without* the liquor.
- *A Twiggy*. Diet soda in a tall glass with plenty of ice.

There are low calorie hors d'oeuvres listed on page 123 of the Calorie Counter which will prevent that hung-over feeling when you step on your scale. If you must dip, use the same cracker over again. The cracker will tend to get soggy after a while. For better results take a small square of linoleum or a mah jong tile along to parties for dipping. (I'm joking, of course!)

Dieting at a dinner party in someone's home particularly on an *On/Diet* day may present problems. When the invitation is extended, tell your hostess that you are on a diet or try to change the date to an *Off/Diet* day. If neither is possible you must really be cautious. Since most hostesses do not offer a choice of menus, as restaurants do, you must plan ahead by saving most of your daily calorie quota for the possibility of a calorie-laden dinner. Even then you don't have to eat everything that is served. When I'm offered something that will send me well over my daily calorie quota, I say, very seriously, "It's very bad for my fatonmythigh." What is "fatonmythigh?" It's a wonderful word to use at parties when you don't want people to know you're dieting. The word sounds so medical and so serious your hostess and other guests will never dare ask you what it is! Actually, it's an affliction which has plagued me all my life:

FAT ON MY THIGH!

When I have a dinner party I plan my menu with calories in mind. I usually serve fish, or a simple chicken dish, or a veal roast with a huge salad made with lots of low-calorie vegetables and a light, vinegary dressing. My hors d'oeuvres are usually celery and carrot sticks, raw stalks of broccoli and cauliflower buds for dipping into cottage cheese that is spiked with minced scallions. I've eliminated filling hot canapes because they often spoil appetites for dinner. I stopped serving bread and butter and I don't believe anyone has missed them. People rarely enjoy that "Oh, am I stuffed" feeling. Even my skinny friends welcome fresh fruit desserts. They have expressed their appreciation of my lower calorie dinners because that's the way they usually eat. (How do you think they stay so skinny?)

No matter how or where you socialize, sandwich yourself between friends and chat more, chew less. Try to relax with the folks at hand, not with the food in mouth. Food does not a good time make. People do!

13

Healthful Eating and the *On/Off Diet*

The *On/Off Diet* is not restrictive. It does not require you to eat *only* protein or *only* rice or *only* anything! Your meals can be well-balanced and health building. Your menus can be nutritious as well as delicious!

On the *Mame* tour I became the Carrie Nation of the coffee shops, brandishing my verbal ax at members of the cast and crew whose daily menus were composed almost entirely of highly processed, non-nutritious foods. I saw it as my personal crusade to keep color in the cheeks, vitality in the steps, and sparkle in the hearts of our little theatrical band who were growing a bit ragged from months on the road.

I felt my perfect record of never having missed a performance (at closing night after 13 months, 383 shows, 110 cities, over 25,000 miles) had given me the right to hawk and pitch my own brand of elixir—*health foods*. My battle cry: "Mens sana in corpore sano!" (A healthy mind in a healthy body!) could be heard from one end of a lunch counter to the other.

As we traveled along the highways on tour there would be signs cautioning against littering and urging us to "Keep America Beautiful!" What about the "litter" we toss into ourselves? Let's keep *Americans* beautiful too! Keep them healthy, keep them youthful, keep them vigorous with foods that nourish rather than rob the body of essential nutrients. To look alive, to feel alive, and to be alive, let us eat live foods.

Some us do not even know what real, live food tastes like: the sweetness of a tree-ripened, unsprayed grapefruit, the tenderness of a fresh-killed, corn-fed chicken, the hearty texture and flavor of whole-grain breads. I have actually known children who at the age of ten have yet to taste a raw tomato. Their tomato eating is confined to pizzas, spaghetti sauces, and ketchup. These are not children from poverty areas, either!

Pollution thrives in America in more ways than one. We pollute our atmosphere, our waters, and our land. When we mar a magnificent natural setting, we very often pollute ourselves as well. Too many suburbs are no longer green but greasy, girdled by tightly clustered concrete and plastic stands with blinding neon signs blazening their wares, huckstering: hamburgers, hot dogs, french fries, fried shrimp, fried chicken, pizza, donuts, frozen custard, and dry cleaning. Their smells meld and hang over these areas in giant, grey, noxious globs. Most of our food today tastes as if it had actually been to the cleaners because it is so filled with chemical additives.

Labels on food read like those of cleaning solutions: propylene glycol, aldehydes, ethyl butyrate, diacetyl, sodium caseinate, carrageen, polysorbate 60, sorbitan monosterate, mono and diglycerides annato. *These are from only three labels*! Just as you read labels when buying clothes, read labels when purchasing food. Here's an easy rule: If you can't pronounce it, don't eat it!

When the label says "Fortified", ask how? "Enriched" — with what? Referring to "enriched" breads and flours, Dr. E. V. McCollum of Johns Hopkins University said: "In the manufacture of white flour a score or more of essential nutrients present in significant amounts in the wheat kernel are removed. To give such flour supplied with three vitamins and iron so good a name as 'enriched' is misleading." In ancient times bread was truly the staff of life for it contained essential B vitamins and minerals. Whole-grain breads are live foods, most other kinds merely litter.

As a child, although our meals were always well-balanced and nutritious, I ate too much, too often. However, as a teenager and young adult I leaned heavily on empty caloried snacks to augment and sometimes substitute for wholesome meals. When I married I ran rampant in my own kitchen, selecting foods for taste rather than wholesomeness. I almost completely abandoned nourishing foods for low-nutritive foods: pasta and other starches, rich pastries, thick sauces, sweets, chips, cookies, and all the other highly processed snacks that *obesies'* tables are laden with. *Because someone eats a lot does not mean that he is well-nourished.* Many *obesies* are undoubtedly among those Americans whom Dr. H. Curtis Wood speaks of in his book *Overfed But Undernourished*. I certainly was!

My dormant knowledge of nutrition was re-awakened when collaborating with Judith Keith on *I Haven't A Thing To Wear*. Judy had always been a health enthusiast and her studio shelves were brimming over with books on health and nutrition. I read and read and then read some more. Slowly I returned to eating highly nutritious, health-building foods.

Staying healthy on a rigorous tour of one-night stands was not easy, however, We moved so fast at times it seemed we did the first act in one town and the second act in another! Finding nutritious foods such as whole-grain breads, broiled meats and poultry, fresh vegetables and fruit is impossible in many restaurants.

Most of our foods suffer losses of essential nutrients through premature harvesting and long periods of storage. Improper kitchen preparation and cooking pour important vitamins and minerals down the drain or into the garbage pail. This is in addition to the devitalization done by processing: canning, freezing, preserving, and smoking. No wonder so much of the food we eat today has about as much nourishment as a Q-Tip! That's why when we arrived in a new town I would check the telephone book and let my fingers do the walking to the nearest health food store.

I would pounce upon the local health hut in search of natural or organic foods. "Organically raised" refers to foods that have not been subjected to chemical fertilizers, sprays, injections, or additives. "Natural foods" are not necessarily organic but they are live—unprocessed and as close to the natural state as possible.

Health foods are not medicine, nor do they taste like medicine. They taste far better than processed foods because they are natural. Whole-grain bread and natural brown rice with none of their vitamins removed are far nuttier, crunchier, and tastier than their processed white facsimilies. Nor are health foods new. They are in fact very old-fashioned. Until fifty years ago everyone was eating them. Breads were made of whole grains. There were little or no chemicals added to our meats, poultry, and fish. Almost all vegetables were eaten fresh (canning was very limited, commercial freezing unknown) and practically everything including sweets and treats was made by Mother in her own kitchen from natural ingredients usually obtained from her own garden or a nearby farm.

You may think that only weirdos or hippies eat health foods today. This is not so. There is a *general trend* back to natural eating. Remember when yogurt was unheard of in regular supermarkets? And then we all became "cultured" by Dannon and other yogurt makers. Now yogurt is ubiquitous and so are many other foods that are good for your family. There is probably a Health Food Section in your own supermarket or a health food store in a nearby shopping center. Health food restaurants are sprouting up everywhere too.

Fun food need not necessarily be litter foods. Cakes and cookies made from natural ingredients such as whole-grain flour, raw sugar or honey, organic fruits, etc. are often tastier than their highly processed relatives. An organic sesame and raisin bar is a wonderful and wholesome snack. A scoop of goat's milk ice cream made with honey and served in a whole-wheat cone is like getting a double dip: one filled with lots of flavor, the other with lots of nourishment.

Raw sugar tastes just as good as white. One tablespoon of raw sugar offers traces of vitamins B1, B2, Niacin, phosphorous, and iron as well as 10 milligrams of calcium. White sugar's vitamin rating is zero, in addition to being a vitamin B and calcium antagonist. Honey, maple syrup, and molasses are also wonderfully nutritious substitutes for white sugar.

Substitutions of natural foods for the processed variety need not be limited only to sweets. Instead of buying bottled or frozen orange juice, I squeeze my own. I get more natural vitamin C that way. Try fresh fruits and vegetables instead of frozen or canned, natural cheeses instead of processed, and homemade soups, breads, and cakes.

Certain natural foods, while nutritious, are high in calories. Therefore, on your *On Diet* days be sparing with: natural sweets, including honey and molasses, whole-wheat cakes, cookies, breads, nuts, natural rice, kasha, seeds, cereals, solid cheeses, wheat germ, oils and rich fruits such as figs,

80 / Candy, Chocolate, Ice Cream and How to Lick 'em!

dates, raisins, and bananas. Natural foods that are low in calories and high in nutrition and therefore good for *On Diet* days are: most other fruits, vegetables, cottage cheese, fish, eggs, plain yogurt.

We all wish to live longer and healthier lives, of course, but we need not severely restrict our pleasures in the attempt. What would an Italian Street Fair be without sausages, zeppole, spumoni? Baskin-Robbins doesn't make a goat's milk ice cream... yet. Why not enjoy a piece of pizza, a slice of chocolate cake, a Nathan's frankfurter? You can have your fun foods in any form if you are certain that your diet includes the Basic Four food groups in the amounts nutritionists state are necessary every day for the maintenance of good health. These Basic Four are:

>1. *Protein.* Six ounces meat, fish, or poultry; or three eggs; or three ounces cheese; or one and a half cups soy beans.

>2. *Fresh Fruits and Fresh Vegetables.* Four servings fruit and vegetables. Make certain to include one citrus fruit, one dark green or leafy vegetable, and one yellow vegetable daily. (A serving is one fruit, or one cup berries, cherries, etc., or $1/2$ cantaloupe, or $1/4$ honeydew; or $1/2$ cup cooked vegetables, or one cup raw greens.)

>3. *Whole-Grain Breads, Cereals, Potatoes, or Natural Rice.* Four servings (A serving is a slice of bread or a muffin, $1/2$ cup potatoes or rice, one cup whole-grain raw cereal or $1/2$ cup cooked cereal.) Whole-grain products provide the all-important B vitamins, lots of them! They also provide calories, lots of them! Therefore, I limit my intake to one or two servings a day and supplement my diet with vitamin B-filled Brewer's Yeast which is only 10 calories per teaspoon.

4. *Milk And Milk Products*. Two servings milk or other dairy products for adults; three to four servings for children and teens. (A serving is eight ounces skimmed or whole milk or one ounce chesse, or $1/2$ cup cottage cheese.)

The Basic Four food groups include all the nutritive elements, vitamins and minerals our bodies thrive on.

We are a nation of "doers" and all too often "over-doers." We over-eat, over-drink, over-smoke, over-work, and overall over-tax ourselves. We, therefore, require food that is over-abundant in nourishment. But what do we do? We over-refine, over-chop, over-peel, over-cook our food into mush instead. To make certain that I get all the essentials I need each and every day, I take vitamin and mineral supplements even though my diet includes many natural foods. Because it is very difficult to know exactly how much nourishment I am actually getting in the foods I buy, vitamin and mineral supplements are like insurance—with me as the beneficiary, reaping the dividends of glowing good health and a younger-looking, more vigorous me!

I'm not tired, I'm not tense. I feel terrific. I am now able to soar through a day where I used to sag in the middle. I almost enjoy exercising, which is a major phenomenon since I was always the reluctant hiker, the retarded gymnast, and the reclining skiier. Now I walk everywhere I can. I use stairs instead of elevators. On some weekends I ride a bike in Central Park. Other times I'm at the seashore swimming or in the country jogging.

The "Loneliness of the Long Distance Runner" can be alleviated by companionship. Why not join a jogging group or have a family circle jog-in? Swim at the Y with friends or join a health, tennis, or golf club.

Some women love massages. As far as I'm concerned, when I get touched like that, I want to be kissed! Some feel it is utterly relaxing and the only exercise they need. It does stimulate circulation and it may promote muscle tone. Does it take off weight? Sure, but only off the masseuse! Massage won't take the place of a reducing diet.

Good health is not an elusive stroke of luck which blesses some and overlooks others. Good health is the absence of pain—physical pain and mental pain. It is a state of mind and body that must be maintained daily, deliberately through wholesome eating.

As we mature we need not grow old or sick. My Aunt Beck, my own "Auntie Mame" is a zippy octogenarian whose motto is "You're only *old* once!" If you really believe as she does, then you'll never be old at all!

On my last birthday my mother called and asked, "How old are we? You've been lying for so long and I've been lying for so long, I can't keep track any more!"

I said, "Mother, you're fifty-five and holding, thanks to proper nutrition and I . . . I feel younger today at thirty than I did ten years ago when I was twenty-nine!" (Well, aren't the best ten years of a woman's life those between twenty-nine and thirty!)

14

Menus and Recipes

Would you believe that there is a bookstore in New York called "Cookbooks Only" which sells only cookbooks (what else?). It has more than 3,000 titles, some dating as far back as 1888. That should give you an idea of the number of books published each year on the subject of food alone!

In addition, women's magazines regularly run recipes and menu sections and feature special diets (high protein, low carbohydrate, low sodium, low calorie, salt-free, egg-free, wheat-free, low residue, etc.). To all of *this* add the numerous recipe annuals prepared by these magazines and the multitudinous pamphlets published by food manufacturers. *The thought we give to food: that's food for thought!*

This abundance of literature exists because what each of us eats varies as much as our individual personalities and life styles. Who is to say, other than your own taste buds (or your own doctor), what *you* should eat? Certainly the *On/Off Diet* does not demand you eat "only this" or not eat "any of that." As long as it stays within your daily calorie quota and helps to keep you healthy, *you can eat whatever you like!*

The following menus, while very personal, include foods which my friends and I enjoy. They are here merely to illustrate the diversity of their individual tastes and to help you get some ideas for your own meals. Any of them can be modified to fit your personal daily calorie quota and your own food preferences. Simply add or eliminate a complete main dish, a vegetable, drinks, or even just a pat of butter.

The following abbreviations are used throughout:

t. = teaspoon
T. = tablespoon
oz. = ounce or ounces

AN ACTRESS' ON DIET DAY (655 Calories)

Before Rehearsal Breakfast

1 sliced orange (Vitamin C can't be stored by the body. We must have it fresh each day.)	60	
1 slice whole-rye toast	55	
2. T. cottage cheese	30	
Coffee, black, no sugar	0	145

Lunch

Poached egg	80	
1 slice whole-wheat toast	55	
Peach	35	
Tea with lemon	0	170

Pep Break

4 oz. V-8 juice	25	
1 t. brewer's yeast	10	35

Dinner

Large green salad with vinegar	50	
1 cup steamed vegetable (zucchini, asparagus, or spinach)	40	
6 broiled shrimp with garlic powder, paprika and oregano, lemon juice	75	
1/3 cup fresh fruit	40	
Coffee, black, no sugar	0	205

After Learning Lines

The Hauser Nightcap, sipped slowly	100	100
1 T. dry skimmed milk powder added to		
6 oz. hot skimmed milk with		
1 t. honey or molasses		
(Suggested by Gaylor Hauser instead of		
tranquilizers or sleeping pills.)		
Good night! No need to dream of more food		
... zzz ... tomorrow we'll have it ... zzzzzz.		
TOTAL		655

AN ACTRESS' *OFF DIET* DAY (1,935 Calories)

On-the-stage but off-the-diet day

Noon Brunch—served by the leading man

1 cup fresh fruit	115
2 eggs with	160
1 t. safflower oil in teflon pan with	35
1/2 oz. lox (smoked salmon) and	85
1/2 fried onion	30

1 slice pumpernickle (3½ × 3½ × ¼)   25
Coffee, black, no sugar   0   450

Pre-Show Snack

Yogurt—8 oz. plain with   120
1 t. molasses and   10
1 t. wheat germ   40
½ oz. sunflower seeds   100   270

Opening Night Supper

2 Martinis   400
Chicken Kabobs Italian*   480
½ cup natural brown rice with herbs   100
Greens with 1 T. safflower oil and vinegar 150
Banana Daiquiri Ice   85
Coffee, black, no sugar   0
Reviews in the a.m. papers   0   1215
                              TOTAL   1935

Chicken Kabobs Italian — Serves 2 — 480 calories per serving, if made according to the following recipe:

2 whole chicken breasts, skinned, split, and boned (1½ pounds)
1 cup low calorie Italian dressing
2 green peppers, seeded, cut into 1-inch slices
8 fresh medium mushrooms
8 small white onions, peeled, sliced
4 fresh medium tomatoes, quartered
oregano to taste

Cut chicken into 1-inch pieces. Marinate for four hours in

low-calorie Italian dressing in refrigerator. Preheat broiler ten minutes. Steam green peppers, mushrooms, and onions with oregano five minutes. Cover a large baking pan with foil, turn up edges to prevent spilling. On eight 8-inch skewers, alternate chicken pieces with tomatoes, green peppers, onions, and mushrooms. Brush them with the remaining low calorie dressing. Place skewers on lined baking pan. Place under broiler with skewers 3 to 5 inches from heat; broil 7 minutes; turn and brush again with dressing. Broil 7 minutes on other side or until chicken is done but still tender.

AN ACTRESS' *ON DIET* DAY (805 Calories)

Breakfast

4 oz. tomato juice	25	
1/2 cup Granola (natural cereal—what a way to wake up!)	65	
1/2 cup skimmed milk	45	
Coffee, black, no sugar	0	135

Pep Break

Coffee or Vanilla Slim Shake*	45	45

Lunch

3 oz. salmon	120	
Lettuce and green pepper with vinegar or low-calorie dressing	30	
1/2 cantaloupe	30	
Coffee, black, no sugar	0	180

Dinner

3 oz. chicken, broiled with curry powder and garlic	115	
1 small baked potato with	100	
1 t. safflower oil and chopped chives	35	
Large green salad with vinegar and	50	
1/2 tomato	15	
1/2 cup fresh strawberries	30	345

After Acting Class

4 oz. red wine	100	100
TOTAL		805

*Slim Shake

1 cup crushed ice
3 t. non-fat dried milk
1/2 cup water
1/2 t. vanilla extract and/or 1 t. instant coffee
1 packet artificial sweetener

Put ingredients into a blender or better still into a malted machine until ice dissolves and shake thickens.

For variety add 1/2 cup fresh fruit (except fresh pineapple) or 1 t. unsweetened cocoa.

A NEW YORK *OFF DIET* DAY (1,745 Calories)

Some people go on walking tours. I occasionally go on an eating excursion with friends on a sunny Saturday.

4 oz. fresh orange juice in Greenwich Village (from a hippie vendor selling organic juice from his rolling cart)	55

Menus and Recipes / 89

1 hot cheese bagel on Rivington Street on the lower East Side of New York—much more than a bagel (125) not quite a Danish—special, unique.   250

On to *Yonah Schimmel* for

1 kasha knish (kasha is 290 calories for one cup cooked; there is less than one half cup in each knish but we will count it as 150 plus the calories in the pastry surrounding it, which is like an unsweetened popover (60) plus 40 calories for oil, etc. and other extras.)   250

Then up to Third Avenue and 18th Street

1 small Goldberg's pizza (considered the best in New York)   490

1 diet soda (mustn't overdo!)   10

Then retrace our steps to Baskin-Robbins' 14th Street and 1st Avenue store for a double-scoop cone of Jamoca Almond Fudge   310

Next a jog to work off some of the calories to Bloomingdale's at 59th and Third where I spend not a calorie, merely dollars on a new size 12.

After the store closes we drag our parched bodies into Daley's Dandelion for a

1 oz. scotch on the rocks   85

Dinner at Costello's on 44th and Third for

4 ozs. Finnan Haddie   100
Green salad with   50
1 T. oil and vinegar   100
1 cup carrots   45

Coffee, black, no sugar	0
We take the bus home with no stops along the way!	
TOTAL	**1745**

ON DIET DAY FRUIT FAST (900 Calories)

If I'm spending a relaxing Sunday at home, catching up on reading and resting, expending very little energy, I will limit my diet to herb tea and no more than nine fresh fruits. The next morning my digestive system gurgles "Thank you" and so does my scale!

A TRAVELER'S OFF DIET DAY (1,465 Calories)

Breakfast—on the run

4 oz. tomato juice with lemon	30	
1 oz. muenster cheese with	80	
1 slice whole-wheat toast (no butter)	55	
Mint tea, no sugar	0	165

Lunch—on the wing

1 oz. scotch on the rocks	85	
3 oz. roast beef, lean	265	
1 cup string beans, yellow with	35	
1 t. margarine	35	
½ cup creamed potato	125	
½ cup banana custard	125	670

Dinner—back at home

3 oz. swordfish	150
Green salad with Slim 'n Spicy dressing*	50

¼ cup rice with   100
1 t. margarine and herbs
Swedish Omelet dessert**   250
Tea with lemon and honey   20   570

Bedtime

6 oz. pear juice   60   60
                              TOTAL   1465

Slim 'n Spicy Dressing

1 package dry salad dressing mix (garlic, onion, or Italian)
¼ cup vinegar, 2 T. water; shake well, then add 1 T. safflower oil, 5 oz. tomato juice. Shake and serve.

**Swedish Omelet Dessert—Serves 4*

4 eggs, 1½ cups scalded milk, 2 t. butter, 1 t. raw sugar, 1 cup crushed fresh fruit (strawberries, blueberries).
Beat the eggs. Add milk and sugar. Heat a casserole and grease lightly with butter. Pour in mixture. Bake 15 to 20 minutes in hot oven (400°F.) Serve with crushed fruit.

HOMEMAKER'S HIGH ENERGY ON DIET DAY (655 Calories)

Breakfast

½ grapefruit   55
1 poached egg with curry   80
1 rice cake   25
Herb tea, no sugar   0   160

Lunch

¾ cup low fat cottage cheese,   150

½ head lettuce		
with vinegar and basil	30	
1 plum	30	
Mint tea, no sugar	0	210

4:00 p.m.

4 oz. tomato juice, with	25	
1 t. brewer's yeast	10	35

Dinner

1 - 8 oz. glass Jump for Joy Vegetable Juice*	50	
4 oz. broiled flounder, with thyme and tarragon	80	
½ cup green beans mixed with	25	
½ cup mushrooms and	10	
1 T. soy sauce	5	
Applesauce Whip**	35	
Tea, no sugar	0	205

11:00/TV News-time

Vanilla Slim Shake***	45	45
TOTAL		655

Jump for Joy Vegetable Juice—Makes a quart, 190 calories total.

6 large carrots, 3 stalks celery, 2 handfuls parsley, ½ cucumber, ¼ wedge cabbage, 1 green pepper. Place all of above in a vegetable juice extractor, beginning with the celery. (Celery acts as a natural strainer and the juicer is easier to clean.) If you do not have a juicer then you will have to plan on including more salads in your menus.

**Applesauce Whip*—Serve 2—35 calories per serving.

1 envelope low calorie lemon gelatin, ¼ cup unsweetened applesauce. Dissolve gelatin in ½ cup hot water, chill until syrupy. Beat until fluffy (beat in chilled bowl or over cracked ice). Fold in applesauce, scoop into sherbet glasses.

***Vanilla Slim Shake—see page 88.

LADIES WHO LUNCH *OFF DIET* DAY (1,645 Calories)

How can you enjoy a special luncheon and still remain within your daily caloric quota? Budget your calories with a tiny breakfast and a sparse dinner.

Breakfast

4 oz. tomato juice	25	
Coffee, black, no sugar	0	25

Lunch

3 oz. Vodka Martini	200	
6 oz. fresh citrus cup	85	
Stuffed baked chicken* with		
½ cup rice with mushrooms and butter	350	
Roll and 2 t. butter	200	
1 cup carrots and peas with 2 t. butter	195	
Salad with 1 T. dressing	100	
Small ice cream sundae	300	
Coffee, black, no sugar	0	1430

Dinner

Steamed vegetable plate with poached egg (asparagus, beets, string beans, squash)	150

94 / *Candy, Chocolate, Ice Cream and How to Lick 'em!*

Orange Whip**	40	
Tea with lemon	0	190
TOTAL		1645

*Stuffed Baked Chicken — Serves 3 — 350 calories per serving.

3 whole chicken breasts; 2 T. flour; 2 t. salt; 1/2 t. black or red pepper; 2 T. butter; 1 clove garlic, minced; 1/4 cup diced ham; 1/2 pound mushrooms; 1/2 cup shelled green peas; 1 stalk celery; 2 sprigs parsley; 1 bay leaf; 1 cup dry white wine; 1 head lettuce, cut in 6 wedges.

Cut the breasts in half through the breast bone. Wash and dry. Mix the flour, salt, and pepper, rub the chicken with seasoned flour. Melt the butter in a casserole, add the chicken breasts and garlic. Brown lightly on both sides. Cover the chicken breasts with the ham, mushrooms, and peas. Add the celery, parsley, bay leaf, and wine to the casserole and place the lettuce wedges over all. Bake in a 350°F. oven for one hour or until chicken is tender. Serve on 1 1/2 cup cooked rice.

**Orange Whip—Makes one serving

1 envelope low calorie orange gelatin dessert; 2 T. cottage cheese; 1/4 t. nutmeg. Dissolve gelatin in 1/2 cup boiling water; chill until cold and syrupy. Whip with rotary egg beater until fluffy. Blend 2 T. cottage cheese with cinnamon and nutmeg and mix with gelatin. Chill.

CAREER WOMAN'S HIGH-POWERED *ON DIET* DAY
(885 Calories)

Breakfast

2 oz. Farmer cheese on	80
1 rice cake	25

Mint tea, no sugar	0	105

Mid-Morning Picker-Upper

4 oz. apple juice with	65	
1 t. brewer's yeast	10	75

Lunch

1 hard boiled egg diced into	80	
Salad of lettuce, cucumber, tomato, watercress with 1 oz. Slim 'n Spicy dressing*	65	
4 halves of apricots stewed in ginger with lemon	90	
Tea, no sugar	0	235

Afternoon Revitalizer

8 oz. glass buttermilk	90	90

Dinner

4 oz. vegetable juice**	25	
3 oz. chicken livers in	155	
5 T. red wine sauce***	50	
4 stalks broccoli and herbs	45	
4 oz. fresh blueberries and diced fresh pineapple with	55	
¼ cup whipped skim milk fluff	10	340

Bedtime

1 nectarine	40	40
TOTAL		885

96 / Candy, Chocolate, Ice Cream and How to Lick 'em!

Slim 'n Spicy Dressing—see page 91.

**Vegetable Juice*—see page 92.

***Red Wine Sauce*— *approximately 10 calories per T.*

1½ cups dry red wine; 2 T. lemon juice; pinch cloves; pinch ginger; 1 small packet sugar substitute.

Heat wine and other ingredients until just before boiling. Saute chicken livers in 3 T. wine sauce in teflon pan. Pour 2 T. sauce on livers after cooking and serve.

CHILD'S ON DIET DAY (1,005 Calories)

Dieting children require more nourishment than dieting adults. Therefore, their *On Diet* caloric quota should be no less than 1,000 calories.

Breakfast

1 small apple	60	
½ cup cooked or 1 cup dry cereal with	125	
½ cup skimmed milk	45	230

Lunch

6 oz. broiled flounder (no butter)	120	
Salad of lettuce, green pepper, celery, carrots, cabbage with	60	
2 oz. Slim 'n Spicy dressing*	15	
½ cantaloupe	40	235

Afternoon

Slim Shake**	45	
made with strawberries (½ cup)	30	
1 t. honey	20	95

(You could make a chocolate shake but chocolate prevents the absorption of calcium by the body. When you drink chocolate milk you get protein, but not calcium. Remember it this way: pour chocolate in, pour calcium out!)

Dinner

2 oz. breaded veal cutlet,	185	
3 broccoli stalks with 1 t. oil	50	
Fresh corn with 1 t. oil	120	
4 oz. glass skimmed milk	45	
1 butter cookie	45	445
TOTAL		1005

Slim 'n Spicy Dressing—see page 91.

**Slim Shake*—see page 88.

CHILD'S *OFF DIET* DAY (1,940 Calories)

Breakfast

½ grapefruit with	55	
1 t. honey	20	
1 poached egg on	80	
1 whole-wheat waffle with	210	
1 T. real maple syrup	70	
8 oz. glass skimmed milk	85	520

Lunch

3½ oz. tuna fish (½ can) with	170
2 t. mayonnaise	60
2 slices rye bread	110
2 sticks celery	10

2 sour pickles	30	
1 peach	35	
1 whole-wheat peanut butter cookie	50	
8 oz. glass skimmed milk	85	550

Afternoon snack

Milk shake	300	300

Dinner

½ broiled chicken	115	
Carrot sticks	50	
½ cup green beans	15	
Baked potato with	100	
2 pats butter (1 T.)	100	
1 banana (medium)	90	470

Bedtime

10 raw cashews	100	100
TOTAL		1940

REGAL REPASTS *ON DIET* DAY (835 Calories)

Follow us now as we explore an average *On Diet* day and an average *Off Diet* day in the life of some of our average *On/Off* dieters, the Queen of Rumania and her brother, the Queen of Greenwich Village. She is tall and elegant and wants to wear a size 10 dress. He is tall and elegant and wants to wear a size 10 dress, so they each consume no more than 1,800 calories on their *Off Diet* days.

A Royal Breakfast

4 oz. spicy tomato juice cocktail, served in a crystal goblet	25

1 slice unbuttered whole-grain toast, crowned with	55	
1 poached egg	80	
Coffee, black, no sugar	0	160

Lunch

4 oz. pickled herring with onions, on a throne of	105	
lettuce, cucumbers, radishes, raw mushrooms, and low calorie diet dressing	35	
1 pomegranate	75	215

Mid-Afternoon

Mineral water, sparkling (A must after herring!)	5	5

Dinner

2 ½ oz. Sherry (a must after mineral water!)	95	
4 oz. broiled sweetbreads	100	
6 stalks asparagus, studded with	20	
1 t. oil	35	
Green salad with vinegar	50	
1" square Brie cheese with	55	
4 rye crackers	80	
Herb tea with honey (1 t.)	20	455
TOTAL		835

FIT-FOR-A QUEEN *OFF DIET* DAY (1,805 Calories)

Brunch—served on a bed of thirteen mattresses

½ cup stewed prunes	155
2 strips lean bacon, on a hotbed of	100

2 buckwheat pancakes with	120	
2 pats butter (1 T.) and	100	
2 T. maple syrup	140	
8 oz. skimmed milk	85	700

Dinner

1 cup fresh fruit compote	85	
Stuffed marinated mushrooms*	65	
1 T. Ikra (caviar) on 2 crackers	85	
4 oz. white wine, in crystal stemware	100	
Chicken-chestnut stew**	400	
Mamaliga (cornmeal-bread-dish)***	175	
Apple'n spice cake****	195	
Espresso coffee	0	1,105
TOTAL		1,805

*Stuffed mushrooms —Serves 4—65 calories per serving.

18 mushrooms, 1 t. salt; 1/4 t. pepper; 1/2 t. paprika; 2 T. grated onion; 2 T. grated cheese; 1 t. oil. Buy medium sized mushrooms. Wash and dry them, remove the stems and chop them fine. Combine with the salt, pepper, paprika, onion, and cheese. Mix well and stuff the mushroom caps. Oil baking pan and arrange the mushrooms on it. Bake in a 375°F. oven 10 minutes. Spear with picks and serve hot.

**Chicken-Chestnut Stew —Serves 3—400 calories per serving.

2 T. butter; 1- 5-pound fowl, disjointed; 2 onions, chopped; 2 t. salt; 1 1/2 t. paprika; 2 T. tomato paste; 1 1/2 cups water; 1/2 pound uncooked chestnuts, peeled. Melt butter in heavy saucepan; saute chicken and chestnuts until tender. Watch carefully and add water if necessary. Add remaining ingredients and simmer over low heat for 15 minutes.

Mamaliga —Serves 9—175 calories per piece.

1³/₄ cups cornmeal; ¼ cup unsifted flour; 2 T. raw sugar; 3 t. baking powder; ½ t. salt; ½ t. soda; ⅓ cup butter; 1¼ cups buttermilk; 1 egg white. Measure cornmeal, flour, sugar, baking powder, soda, and salt into mixing bowl. Mix well. Add butter and break up with fork. Mix buttermilk with egg white. Add dry ingredients and stir until smooth. Bake in 8 x 8 x 2 inch pan, brushed with margarine. Bake at 450°F. for 25 minutes.

*****Apple 'n Spice Cake*** —Serves 14—195 calories per slice.

½ cup raisins; ½ cup water; 2 cups unsifted flour; ¼ cup raw sugar; ½ t. baking powder; 1 t. soda; ½ t. cloves; ½ t. nutmeg; ¼ t. salt; ½ cup butter; ½ cup finely chopped apple. Simmer raisins in water for 5 minutes. Remove from heat. Measure and add enough water to make 1 cup. Cool. Measure flour, sugar, baking powder, soda, cloves, nutmeg, and salt into mixing bowl. Mix well. Cut in butter with pastry blender or fork until mixture resembles coarse meal. Add apple and raisin mixture to dry ingredients. Stir until thoroughly blended. Pour into 9 × 5 × 3 inch loaf pan brushed with margarine. Bake at 325°F. about one hour or until cake springs back when lightly touched in center. Makes 1 loaf cake.

AN EXECUTIVE'S *ON DIET* DAY (805 Calories)

Mad Dash for the Mad. Ave. Bus Breakfast

4 oz. orange juice	55	
Coffee with 1 oz. skimmed milk	10	65

Lunch

1 Bloody Mary	175

4 oz. broiled scallops	175	
Green salad with lemon	50	400

Dinner

1 Martini	200	
8 Oysters on the half shell with	100	
Cocktail sauce	40	340
TOTAL		805

AN EXECUTIVE'S *OFF DIET* DAY (1,745 Calories)

Breakfast

4 oz. orange juice	55	
Coffee with 1 oz. skimmed milk	10	65

Expense Account Luncheon

2 Bloody Marys	350	
5 oz. (cooked) chopped steak	500	
Spinach salad with bacon dressing	170	1020

Drinks with Clients and Snack before Theater

2 Martinis	400	
1 jumbo shrimp cocktail with	150	
Cocktail sauce	30	580

At Home

Small fruit	80	80
TOTAL		1,745

A SWINGING BACHELOR'S ON DIET DAY
(880 Calories)

The swinging bachelor is a steak and salad man with a few blonds and brunettes thrown in for flavor.

Breakfast

1 English muffin with	125	
1 t. butter	50	
Coffee, black, no sugar	0	
Vitamin and mineral supplements	0	175

Lunch

1 oz. hard cheese	100	100

Dinner

4 oz. (cooked) broiled steak	400	
Green salad with diet dressing	50	
5 oz. frozen strawberries in syrup	155	605
TOTAL		880

A SWINGING BACHELOR'S OFF DIET DAY
(1,900 Calories)

Breakfast

1 hard roll with	125	
1 t. butter	50	
Coffee, black, no sugar	0	
Vitamin and mineral supplements	0	175

Lunch

Bologna (1½ × ½ slice)	235

104 / Candy, Chocolate, Ice Cream and How to Lick 'em!

1 oz. cheddar cheese	70	
2 slices seeded rye bread	110	
1 t. mustard	15	
Diet soda	10	440

Dinner

3 oz. frozen daiquiri	180	
1 cup pop corn without butter	55	
Green salad with diet dressing	50	
7 oz. (cooked) broiled sirloin steak	700	
10 oz. frozen fruit in syrup	300	1,285
TOTAL		1,900

A COMMUTER'S *ON DIET* DAY (815 Calories)

Except for weekday walks between home and garage and garage and office, he is fairly inactive. He prefers saving calories for the evening and his favorite liquid, scotch.

Breakfast

1 sliced orange	60	
2 T. cottage cheese on	60	
Bran muffin	80	
Coffee, black, no sugar	0	
The New York Times	0	200

Lunch

1 container plain yogurt	120	
Pear	95	215

Dinner

2 oz. scotch	170	

¾ lb. lobster, with		90	
Cocktail sauce		30	
Green salad with diet dressing		50	
½ cantaloupe		60	400
	TOTAL		815

A COMMUTER'S OFF DIET DAY (1,780 Calories)

Breakfast

½ grapefruit	55	
Bagel with	125	
2 T. cream cheese	110	
Coffee, black, no sugar	0	290

Lunch

4 oz. pickled herring	105	
Matzoh, 1 piece (4 x 8)	50	
Prune whip yogurt, 1 cup	260	415

Dinner

3 scotches*	255	
2 halves, low calorie deviled eggs à la Karin**	90	
Corned beef, 2 slices (4 x 1½ x 1)	200	
Cabbage, 1 cup, with	40	
½ T. oil	50	
Green salad with diet dressing	50	
Brownie, small	135	820

Watching TV

3 scotches		255	255
	TOTAL		1,780

*The commuter drinks only for medicinal purposes. His doctor told him he has a very small liver and he will drink only until it becomes enlarged enough to be considered normal!

** *Low Calorie Deviled Eggs à la Karin* — each egg (2 halves) 90 calories.

6 eggs; 3 T. cottage cheese; 2 t. tangy ketchup; 1/4 t. horseradish; 1/8 t. pepper; paprika for garnish.

Hard boil six eggs. Cool in cold water. Peel. Slice each egg in half putting yolks in bowl. Set whites to one side. In bowl with yolks add the cottage cheese, ketchup, horseradish, and pepper. Mix well and replace in egg whites. Garnish with paprika.

The Candy, Chocolate, Ice Cream and How to Count 'em Calorie Counter

Contents

Beverages, Alcoholic   111

Beverages, non-Alcoholic   112

Breads, Cereals and Grains   113
    Biscuits and Buns   113
    Breads   113
    Cereals   113
    Crackers   114
    Muffins   114
    Rolls   114
    Other Grains and Grain Products   115

Candy, Sugars, and Sweets   115
    Candy   115
    Sugars   117
    Syrups and Other Sweets   117
    Jams and Jellies   117

Dairy Products   117

Desserts   119
    Cakes   119
    Cookies   120
    Fruit Desserts   120
    Ice Cream Desserts   121
    Pastries   122
    Pies   122
    Puddings   123
    Toppings   123

Dining Out and Party Foods   123
>   Cocktail-hour Appetizers   123
>   Appetizers, Prepared   124
>   Dinner Selections   125
>   Chinese   125
>   Fish and Seafood   125
>   Italian   125
>   Steak   126
>   Sauces   126

Eggs   126

Fats and Oils   126

Fruits   127

Juices   129

Meat, Fish, Seafood, and Poultry   130

Natural and Organic Foods   135

Nuts and Seeds   137

Prepared Foods   137
>   Appetizers   137
>   Meat, Fish and Poultry   138
>   TV Dinners   138

Seasonings, Sauces, and Dressings   138

Soups   140

Vegetables   141

NOTE: The following abbreviations are used:
> t. = teaspoon
> T. = tablespoon
> oz. = ounce or ounces

BEVERAGES, ALCOHOLIC

Ale	8	oz. glass	150
Alexander, Brandy or Gin	3	oz. cocktail	185
Anisette	1	oz. cordial	80
Beer, Bock	8	oz. glass	175
Beer, Lager	8	oz. glass	125
Bloody Mary	8	oz. glass	175
Brandies (Most)	1	oz. cordial	75
Brandy Sour	6	oz. delmonico	155
Champagne, Pink or White	6	oz. glass	150
Champagne Cocktail	6	oz. deep V	175
Cherry Herring	1	oz. cordial	100
Creme de Cocoa, de Menthe	1	oz. cordial	95
Daiquiri	3	oz. cocktail	180
Gin	1	oz. pony	75
Gin Collins	10	oz. glass	155
Gin Fizz	8	oz. highball	135
Manhattan Cocktail	3	oz. cocktail	260
Martini, Regular or Dry	3	oz. cocktail	200
Mint Julep	10	oz. collins	355
Muscatel Wine	4	oz. wineglass	190
Pink Lady	3	oz. cocktail	170
Planter's Punch	10	oz. collins	365
Port Wine	4	oz. wineglass	190
Rum	1	oz. jigger	100
Rye Whiskey	1	oz. jigger	100
Scotch Mist or Sour	6	oz. old fashion	85
Scotch and Soda	8	oz. highball	90
Scotch Whisky	1	oz. jigger	85
Sherry	2½	oz. glass	95
Sloe Gin	1	oz. jigger	55
Sloe Gin Fizz	8	oz. highball	155
Sparkling Burgundy	4	oz. wineglass	100
Stinger	3	oz. cocktail	185
Stout	8	oz. glass	140
Tom Collins	10	oz. glass	155
Tokay Wine	4	oz. wineglass	180
Vermouth, Sweet or Italian	4	oz. wineglass	175
Vodka	1½	oz. jigger	180
Whiskey:			
Canadian	1	oz. pony	100
Irish	1	oz. jigger	100
Scotch	1	oz. jigger	85
Whiskey Highball	8	oz. glass	175
Whiskey Sour	3	oz. cocktail	200
Wine, Dry (Most)	4	oz. wineglass	95
Wine, Sweet (Most)	4	oz. wineglass	130
Zombi	14	oz. glass	510

112 / Candy, Chocolate, Ice Cream and How to Lick 'em!

BEVERAGES, NON-ALCOHOLIC

Buttermilk	8 oz. glass	90
Bitter Lemon	8 oz. glass	105
Bitter Orange	8 oz. glass	125
Carbonated Water (Seltzer)	8 oz. glass	5
Cherry Soda	8 oz. glass	125
Club Soda	8 oz. glass	trace
Chocolate Milk (Whole Milk)	8 oz. glass	185
Chocolate Milk (Skimmed Milk)	8 oz. glass	110
Cider, Apple (Sweet)	8 oz. glass	115
Cocoa (Whole Milk)	8 oz. cup	180
Cocoa (Skimmed Milk)	8 oz. cup	105
Cocoa Dry Powder	3 T.	65
Coconut Milk	8 oz. glass	60
Coffee, Black	8 oz. cup	0
Add the following calories for milk and sugar:		
Sugar	1 t.	20
Light Cream	1 T.	30
Milk, Whole	1 T.	10
Milk, Skimmed	1 T.	10
Cola Beverages	8 oz. glass	100
Cream Soda	8 oz. glass	130
Fruited Soft Drink Mix		
(Kool-Aid, All Flavors)	8 oz. glass	95
Ginger Ale	8 oz. glass	70
Grape Soda	8 oz. glass	130
Ice Cream Soda (Average)	1 fountain serving	300
Instant Breakfast—Straw.,Choc.	1 package	290
Lemonade (Average)	8 oz. glass	100
Malted Milk (Most Flavors)	1 fountain serving	300
Milk, Evaporated (1/2 water)	8 oz. glass	170
Milk, Fat-Free (Skimmed)	8 oz. glass	85
Milk, Goat's	8 oz. cup	165
Milk, Whole	8 oz. glass	165
Milk, 1/2 Cream	8 oz. glass	330
Milk, Skimmed	8 oz. glass	90
Non-Dairy Creamer	1 T.	35
Non-Fat, Milk Solid	1 T.	35
Orange Soda	8 oz. glass	120
Orangeade (Average)	8 oz. glass	100
Ovaltine (Whole Milk)	8 oz. glass	240
Ovaltine (Skimmed Milk)	8 oz. glass	175
Postum or Sanka, Black	8 oz. cup	0
Quinine Water (Schweppes)	8 oz. glass	90
Root Beer	8 oz. glass	100
Sanka	8 oz. cup	0
Soda, Ice Cream (Average)	1 fountain serving	300
Tea	8 oz. cup	0
Tea With Lemon	8 oz. cup	5
Water	a tubful	0

BREADS, CEREALS, AND GRAINS

Biscuits and Buns

Baking Powder	2½" diameter	130
Cinnamon	2½" square	140
Plain	2¾" diameter	125

Breads

Boston Brown	3" × 4" × ½" slice	100
Brown Nut Bread	3" × 4" × ½" slice	100
Cinnamon Toast	4" × 4½" × ½ slice	130
Corn	2" × 2½" × 1½" square	105
Crumbs (Bread)	8 oz. cup	345
Cracked Wheat	3" × 4" × ½" slice	80
Date and Nut	3" × 4" × ½" slice	105
French	3" × 3½" × ½" oval	35
Gluten	3" × 4" × ½" slice	35
Italian	3" × 3½" × ½" oval	35
Melba Toast	3½" × 1½" × ¼" piece	30
Pumpernickel	3½" × 3½" × ¼" slice	25
Raisin	3" × 4" × ½" slice	80
Rye	3½" × 4½" × ½" oval	55
Rye Krisp	3½" × 2" wafer	20
Short Bread	1¾" square	40
Swedish Health	2" square	50
Vienna	3" × 3½" × ½" oval	55
White	4" × 4½" × ½" slice	65
Whole-Wheat	4" × 4½" × ½" slice	55
Whole-Wheat Raisin	4" × 4½ × ½" slice	60

Cereals

All-Bran	8 oz. cup	145
Bran Flakes (40% Bran)	8 oz. cup	135
Bran, Raisin	8 oz. cup	150
Bran, Whole Cereal	8 oz. cup	190
Cereals, Cooked (Average)	8 oz. cup	200
Cheerios Breakfast Cereal	8 oz. cup	100
Corn Flakes (Most Brands)	8 oz. cup	110
Cream of Wheat (Cooked)	8 oz. cup	110
Farina (Cooked)	8 oz. cup	105
Granola	1 oz.	135
Grapenuts Breakfast Cereal	8 oz. cup	400
Kellogs 'K' Cereal	8 oz. cup	180
Oatmeal (Cooked)	8 oz. cup	140
Post Toasties Cereal	8 oz. cup	110
Puffed Rice (Most Brands)	8 oz. cup	55
Rice Flakes (Most Brands)	8 oz. cup	120
Rice Krispies	8 oz. cup	125
Rolled Oats	8 oz. cup	100
Rye Flakes	8 oz. cup	125

114 / Candy, Chocolate, Ice Cream and How to Lick 'em!

Shredded Wheat (Biscuit)	2½" × 2" square	80
Shredded Wheat (Bite Size)	8 oz. cup	215
Wheat Flakes	8 oz. cup	125
Wheat Germ	8 oz. cup	245
Wheat, Puffed (Most Brands)	8 oz. cup	145
Wheatena (Cooked)	8 oz. cup	120
Wheaties	8 oz. cup	125

Crackers

Animal	6 pieces	50
Butter	2" diameter	20
Cheese	2" square	25
Graham	1 piece	30
Matzoh	4" × 8" piece	50
Melba	3½" × 1½" × ¼ piece	20
Oyster	10 small pieces	45
Pretzels (Reg. Twist Size)	3 pretzels	50
Pretzel Sticks	7 sticks	20
Ritz	2" diameter	15
Rye Krisp	3½" × 2" piece	20
Rye Wafers	3¼" × 1¾" oblong	15
Saltines	2" square	70
Soda (Medium or 2 Small)	2½" square	25
Triscuits	4 average pieces	90
Whole Wheat	2¾" × 2" oblong	35

Muffins

Blueberry	2½" diameter	130
Bran	3½" diameter	80
Cornmeal	2¾" diameter	135
Date	2¾" diameter	140
English	3½" diameter	125
Plain	2¾" diameter	135
Raisin	3½" diameter	130
Rye	2¾" diameter	135
White (Plain)	2¾" diameter	135
Whole Wheat	2¾" diameter	130

Rolls

Bagels	1 med.	125
Cheese Bagel	1	250
French (Hard Roll)	3½" diameter	100
Hamburger	3½" diameter	155
Hot Dog	6" × 1¾" diameter	160
Onion	4" diameter	150
Parker House	2¾" diameter	125
Plain	2¾" diameter	125
Sweet	3½" diameter	135

Other Grains and Grain Products

Barley, Pearled (Light-Dry)	8 oz. cup	710
Barley Cereal	4 T.	90
Bran, Raisin	8 oz. cup	150
Bran, Whole Cereal	8 oz. cup	150
Buckwheat Flour	8 oz. cup	340
Cereals (see individual cereals)		
Corn Flour (Dry-sifted)	8 oz. cup	400
Corn Grits (Cooked)	8 oz. cup	120
Cornmeal (Cooked)	8 oz. cup	120
Cracked Wheat	8 oz. cup	155
Hominy Grits (Cooked)	8 oz. cup	125
Kasha (Cooked)	8 oz. cup	290
Kasha Knish	1 large	290
Macaroni (Cooked)	8 oz. cup	210
Macaroni with Cheese	8 oz. cup	465
Noodles (Cooked)	8 oz. cup	200
Pancakes, Buckwheat	4" diameter (1 oz.)	60
Pancakes, French	4" diameter (1 oz.)	65
Pancakes, Griddle	4" diameter (1 oz.)	60
Pancakes, Wheat	4" diameter (1 oz.)	60
Rice, Brown (Dry)	8 oz. cup	750
Rice, Fried (Cooked)	8 oz. cup	260
Rice, Spanish (Cooked)	8 oz. cup	300
Rice, White (Cooked)	8 oz. cup	200
Rice, Wild (Dry)	8 oz. cup	600
Rye Flour (Light)	8 oz. cup	285
Spaghetti (Canned)	8 oz. cup	245
Spaghetti (Cooked)	8 oz. cup	270
Spaghetti, with Meat Sauce	1/2 cup (4 oz.)	200
Spaghetti, with Tomato Sauce	1/2 cup (4 oz.)	190
Soybean Flour (Dry)	8 oz. cup	230
Tortillas	5" diameter	50
Wheat, Cracked	8 oz. cup	175
Wheat, Rolled (Cooked)	8 oz. cup	180
Wheat Flour (All Purpose)	8 oz. cup	400
Wheat Flour (All Purpose)	1 T.	30
Wheat Germ	8 oz. cup	245
Wild Rice Shoots	8 oz. cup	225
Waffles	1/2" × 4 1/2" × 5 1/2"	210

CANDY, SUGARS AND SWEETS

Candy

Almond Joy	1 1/2 oz. (2 pieces)	220
Bon Bons	1" round piece	75
Butterscotch	1" square piece	75
Candy, Hard	1 oz.	110
Caramels, Plain or Nuts	1" square (1 oz.)	125

116 / Candy, Chocolate, Ice Cream and How to Lick 'em!

Chocolate Bar, Plain or Nuts (Average)	2 oz. bar	260
Chocolate, Bitter (Unsweetened)	1 oz. piece	140
Chocolate Creams	1 oz. piece	110
Chocolate Fudge	1 oz. piece	115
Chocolate Mints	1 oz.	110
Chocolate, Semi-Sweet	1 oz. piece	145
Chocolate, Sweet	1 oz. piece	155
Chocolate, Sweet with Nuts	1 oz. piece	170
Coconut Creams	1" square piece	100
Cough Drops (Average)	1 drop	10
Dates, Pitted or Stuffed	1 oz.	45
Forever Yours	1 oz.	100
Fruit Drops (Varied Flavors)	3 med. drops	100
Glazed Fruit (Varied Types)	1 oz.	95
Gum, Candy Coated (Average)	2 pieces	15
Gum, Chewing (Most Flavors, Average)	1 stick	10
Gum Drops (Varied Flavors)	1 large or 6 small pieces	35
Halvah	1¼ oz. piece	125
Hard Candy (Varied Flavors)	1 oz.	110
Hershey Bar	1 oz.	155
Hershey Bar with Almonds	1 oz.	155
Hershey Kisses	1 oz.	155
Kisses, Taffy (Average)	3 pieces (1 oz.)	100
Lemon Drops	3 med. drops	100
Life Savers, Hole Type (All Flavors)	1 piece	5
Life Savers, Solid Type (All Flavors)	1 piece	10
Lollipops (All Flavors)	1 oz.	110
Maple Sugar	2" patty (1 oz.)	110
Marshmallows, Chocolate	1 oz.	105
Marshmallow, Plain	1 oz.	90
Milky Way	1 oz.	110
Mints, After Dinner, Chocolate	3" dia. piece (1 oz.)	110
Mints, After Dinner, Plain	½" dia. piece	10
Mounds	1 oz.	125
Nougats, Plain or Nuts	1" square (1 oz.)	120
O'Henry	1 oz.	130
Peanut Bar (Average)	2 oz. bar	260
Peanut Brittle	1 oz. piece	125
Popcorn, Crackerjack Type	1 box	250
Powerhouse	1 oz.	110
Praline (Most Types)	3" diameter piece	300
Sour Balls (Most Flavors, Average)	1 piece	20
Sugar Apple	1	195
Taffy, Kisses or Nougats (Average)	3 pieces (1 oz.)	100
Toffee, English or Coffee (Average)	1 piece	25
Tootsie Roll (Average)	1 bar	110

Sugars

Beet Sugar	1 t.	20
Brown Sugar	1 t.	20
Cane Sugar	1 t.	20
Cube Sugar	1¼" × ¾" × ½"	30
Dextro-Maltose	1 T.	40
Granulated Sugar	1 t.	20
Powdered Sugar	1 T.	30
Sugar, Beet	1 t.	20
Sugar Cane, Peeled Stalks	3½ oz.	50
Sugar, Maple	1 T.	60

Syrups and Other Sweets

Black Raspberry Topping (Kraft)	1 T.	40
Butterscotch Topping (Hershey's)	1 T.	55
Cane Syrup	1 T.	60
Caramel Topping (Smucker's)	1 T.	50
Chocolate Fudge Topping (Hershey's)	1 T.	60
Chocolate Syrup	1 T.	45
Corn Syrup	1 T.	60
Hard Sauce	1 T.	65
Honey	1 T.	65
Maple Syrup (Pure)	1 T.	70
Maple Syrup (Imitation)	1 T.	65
Marshmallow Cream Topping	1 T.	45
Molasses, Cane (Light)	1 T.	50
Molasses, Cane (Medium)	1 T.	45
Molasses, Cane (Blackstrap)	1 T.	45
Pecans in Syrup	1 T.	90
Pineapple Syrup	1 T.	40
Simple Syrup	1 T.	60
Strawberry Syrup	1 T.	50
Syrups, (Most Table Blends)	1 T.	60
Syrups, Sugar Cane	3 fl. oz.	60

Jams and Jellies

Apple Butter	1 T.	35
Cranberry Jelly	1 T.	25
Cranberry Sauce (Sweetened)	8 oz. cup	50
Fruit Jellies (Most Flavors)	1 T.	50
Jams (Most Flavors)	1 T.	55
Marmalade	1 T.	55

DAIRY PRODUCTS

American Cheese	1 slice (1 oz.)	100

118 / Candy, Chocolate, Ice Cream and How to Lick 'em!

American Cheese (Grated)	1 T.	30
Blue Cheese	1 T.	55
Brie	1" square	100
Butter, Salt	1 patty (1 t.)	50
Butter, Sweet	1 patty (1 t.)	50
Buttermilk	8 oz. glass	90
Camembert, Cheese	1 triangle (1 oz.)	85
Chateau Cheese	1 oz. piece	100
Cheddar Cheese	1" cube (1 oz.)	70
Chocolate Milk (Whole)	8 oz. glass	185
Chocolate Milk (Skimmed)	8 oz. glass	110
Cocoa (with Whole Milk)	8 oz. cup	180
Cocoa (with Skimmed Milk)	8 oz. cup	110
Cocoa Malt	8 oz. glass	280
Condensed Milk (Sweetened)	1 T.	65
Condensed Milk (Unsweetened)	1 T.	25
Cottage Cheese, Creamed	8 oz. cup	215
Cottage Cheese, Uncreamed	8 oz. cup	195
Cream Cheese	1 T.	55
Cream Cheese Spreads (Average)	1 oz.	95
Cream, Non-Dairy	1 T.	35
Cream, Light	1 T.	30
Cream, Heavy	1 T.	50
Cream, Sour	1 T.	60
Edam Cheese	1 oz. scoop	120
Eggnog	8 oz. glass	270
Evaporated Milk (Unsweetened)	1 T.	20
Farmer Cheese	4 oz. piece	155
Feta Cheese	1 oz. portion	90
Goat's Milk	8 oz.	165
Gorgonzola Cheese	1 oz. piece	100
Grated Romano	1 T.	30
Gruyere Cheese	1 slice (1 oz.)	100
Liederkranz Cheese	2 T.	100
Limburger Cheese	2 T.	100
Malted Milk (Most Flavors)	10 oz. fountain glass	595
Milk, Acidophilus	8 oz. glass	100
Milk, Skimmed	8 oz. glass	90
Milk, Whole (Grade A)	8 oz. glass	165
Neufchatel Cheese	1 oz.	100
Old English Cheese Spread	2 T.	100
Olive Pimento Spread	2 T.	90
Ovaltine (with Skimmed Milk)	8 oz. glass	175
Ovaltine (with Whole Milk)	8 oz. glass	240
Parmesan Cheese (Grated)	1 T.	30
Pot Cheese	4 oz.	65
Provolone Cheese	2 T.	100
Roquefort Cheese	1" square (1 oz.)	105
Sour Cream	2 T.	120
Swiss Cheese	1 slice (1 oz.)	105
Swiss Gruyere Cheese	1 slice (1 oz.)	100

Velveeta Cheese	2 slices (1 oz.)	100
Welsh Rarebit Sauce	8 oz. cup	200
Yogurt, Plain	8 oz. cup	120
Yogurt, Flavored		
Apricot (Dannon)	1/2 cup	130
Banana (Dannon)	1/2 cup	130
Blueberry (Breakstone)	1/2 cup	145
Coffee (Dannon)	1/2 cup	100
Mandarin Orange (Borden)	1/2 cup	135
Pineapple (Breakstone)	1/2 cup	145
Prune Whip (Dannon)	1/2 cup	130
Raspberry (Borden)	1/2 cup	140
Strawberry (Borden)	1/2 cup	135
Vanilla	1/2 cup	130

DESSERTS

Cakes

Almond Cake	3" × 2" × 3/4" piece	175
Angel Cake	1/12 of 8" diameter	110
Apple Crumb	1 med. piece	170
Apple Turnover	1 med. piece	275
Butter Cake	3" × 3 1/2" × 1/2" piece	200
Caramel Cake (Incl. Icing)	3" × 3 1/2" × 1/2" piece	175
Cheesecake	3" × 2" × 1 1/2" piece	300
Cheesecake, Pineapple	3" × 2" × 1 1/2" piece	310
Chocolate Eclair, Cream	1 med. piece	300
Chocolate Eclair, Custard	1 med. piece	250
Chocolate Layer, (Incl. Icing)	1" × 1 1/2" × 1" piece	155
Coconut Cake	3" wedge	250
Coffee Cake	3 1/2" wedge	260
Cup Cake (No Icing)	1 3/4" diameter	145
Devil's Food Cake	3" × 2" × 3/4" piece	150
Donut, Solid (with Filling Average)	1 med.	200
Donut, Hole Type (Incl. Icing, Average)	1 med.	150
Fruit Cake	2" × 2" × 1/2" piece	115
Ginger Cake	2" × 2" × 2" piece	175
Gold Cake	3" × 2" × 1 1/2" piece	180
Griddle Cake	(Refer to "Pancakes")	
Ice Box Cake	2" × 2" × 3/4" piece	235
Jelly Roll	1 slice 1/2" thick	150
Layer, Two (Incl. Icing)	2" × 1 1/2" × 1" piece	100
Pancakes, Wheat/Buckwheat	4" diameter	60
Pound Cake	2 3/4" × 3" × 5/8"	140
Popover	3" diameter	60
Short Cake, Plain	3" × 3" × 2" square	145
Sponge Cake	1/12th of 8" diameter	120
Strawberry Short Cake	3" × 3" × 2" square	320
Vanilla Plain (No Icing)	2" × 2" × 1" piece	100
Vanilla (Incl. Icing)	2" × 1 1/2" × 1" piece	100

Cookies

Brownies	2" ×2" × 3/4"	135
Butter	2" diameter	45
Chocolate	2" diameter	75
Chocolate Chip	2" diameter	50
Chocolate Marshmallow	2" diameter	80
Cookies, Plain or Assorted (Average)	3" diameter	100
Cookies, Wafers	2¼" diameter	50
Fig Newton	1 large piece	90
Ginger Snaps	3" diameter	30
Graham, Chocolate, Covered	2½" square	45
Graham Cracker (Medium)	3½" square	25
Graham Cracker (Small)	2½" square	15
Honey	3½" diameter	50
Lorna Doone	2" square	35
Macaroons	2½" diameter	50
Oat	2½" diameter	50
Oatmeal	3" diameter	60
Oreo Sandwich	2" diameter	55
Petite Fours	1 average piece	150
Social Tea	2¼" × 1½" oblong	25
Soya	1½" square	10
Sugar	3½" diameter	45
Vanilla	3½" diameter	50

Fruit Desserts

Apple, Baked	1 med.	75
Apple Betty	8 oz. cup	345
Apple dumpling (Average)	1 med.	300
Applesauce (Sweetened)	½ cup (4 oz.)	95
Applesauce (Unsweetened)	½ cup (4 oz.)	50
Apricots, Canned in Syrup	4 med. halves	100
Apricots, Fresh	3 med.	55
Bananas, Sliced	8 oz. cup	135
Blackberries, Fresh	8 oz. cup	85
Blueberries, Fresh	8 oz. cup	85
Cantaloupe	½ of 5" diameter	40
Cherries, Canned	8 oz. cup	125
Figs, Stewed	2 large	115
Fruit Cocktail, Canned	8 oz. cup	175
Fruit Cocktail, Fresh	¾ cup (6 oz.)	85
Grapefruit, Fresh	½ of 4¼" med.	75
Orange, Fresh	3" diameter med.	70
Orange and Grapefruit Sections	8 oz. cup	85
Peach, Fresh	2½" × 2" diameter	45
Peaches, Canned in Syrup	8 oz. cup	175
Pears, Canned in Syrup	8 oz. cup	175
Pineapple, Canned in Syrup	1 large slice	95
Pineapple, Fresh (Slice)	3½" diameter × 3/4"	45
Prunes (with Sugar Added)	½ cup (4 oz.)	245

115 — bread
170 — tuna
35 — mayo.
100 — O.J.

420

680 — las.
30 — lettuce
65 — Dressing
90 — milk

1,285
50

1,335
90

1,425   1,685

100 - 0.T.
Tuna - 170
Mayo - 35
Lettuce - 10

315

115
170
35
85

405

Sat.
10-0
7

1050

400
405

260

665

335 more

900
315

585

585
LEFT

Raspberries, Black	1 cup (8 oz.)	100
Raspberries, Red	1 cup (8 oz.)	70
Rhubarb, Stewed with Sugar	1 cup (8 oz.)	385
Strawberries, Fresh	1 cup (8 oz.)	55
Watermelon	1/2 of 10″ diameter × 3/4″	45

Ice Cream Desserts

Banana Ice Cream	1 scoop (1/2 cup)	290
Banana Split	fountain size	1,165
Baskin-Robbins Ice Cream Flavors	1/2 cup scoop	
Banana Daiquiri Ice		85
Butter Pecan		150
Chocolate Fudge		185
Chocolate Mint		145
French Vanilla		175
Fresh Peach		120
Fresh Strawberry		135
Here Come Da Fudge		155
Jamoca		140
Jamoca Almond Fudge		155
Mango Sherbert		95
Rocky Road		160
Black and White Soda	fountain size	310
Butter Almond Ice Cream	1 scoop (1/2 cup)	300
Butter Pecan Ice Cream	1 scoop (1/2 cup)	300
Butterscotch Ice Cream	1 scoop (1/2 cup)	395
Cherry Ice	1 scoop (1/2 cup)	120
Cherry Ice Cream	1 scoop (1/2 cup)	295
Cherry Vanilla Ice Cream	1 scoop (1/2 cup)	295
Chocolate Chip Ice Cream	1 scoop (1/2 cup)	300
Chocolate Ice Cream	1 scoop (1/2 cup)	300
Chocolate Ice Cream Soda	fountain size	320
Chocolate Sundae	fountain size	300
Coffee Ice Cream	1 scoop (1/2 cup)	295
Coffee Ice Cream Soda	fountain size	310
Cone, Ice Cream (without Ice Cream)	1	45
Custard, Frozen	1 scoop (1/2 cup)	150
Fudge Ice Cream Pop	1 avg. size	320
Fudge Sundae (Average)	fountain size	300
Fudge, Hot Sundae (Average)	fountain size	310
Lemon Ice	1 scoop (1/2 cup)	115
Malted Milk (Most Flavors)	fountain size	600
Milk Shake (Most Flavors)	fountain size	305
Maple Walnut Sundae	fountain size	300
Marshmallow Sundae	fountain size	300
Nesselrode Ice Cream	1 scoop (1/2 cup)	300
Orange Ice	1 scoop (1/2 cup)	120
Pineapple Ice	1 scoop (1/2 cup)	120
Pineapple Ice Cream	1 scoop (1/2 cup)	250
Pineapple Ice Cream Soda	fountain size	315
Pineapple Sundae	fountain size	305

122 / Candy, Chocolate, Ice Cream and How to Lick 'em!

Pistachio Ice Cream	1 scoop (½ cup)	255
Pop, Ice Cream (with Coating, Most Flavors)	1 avg.	200
Raspberry Ice	1 scoop (½ cup)	120
Raspberry Ice Cream	1 scoop (½ cup)	300
Sandwich, Ice Cream	1 average	255
Sugar Cone (without Ice Cream)	1	45
Tutti Frutti Ice Cream	1 scoop (½ cup)	260
Vanilla Ice Cream	1 scoop (½ cup)	285
Vanilla Fudge Ice Cream	1 scoop (½ cup)	295
Vanilla Malted (with Ice Cream)	fountain size	600
Vanilla Milk Shake	fountain size	305
Vanilla Pop, Chocolate Covering	1 regular size	140
Vanilla Soda, Plain	fountain size	150
Vanilla Soda, Ice Cream	fountain size	315
Walnut Ice Cream	1 scoop (½ cup)	280
Walnut Sundae	fountain size	300

Pastries

Apple Turnover	1 med. piece	275
Chocolate Eclair, Cream	1 med.	300
Chocolate Eclair, Custard	1 med.	250
Cream Puff, Chocolate	1 med.	315
Danish Pastry (Average)	1 med.	200 to 300
French Pastry (Average)	1 med.	175 to 275
Jelly Roll	1 slice ½" thick	150
Lady Fingers	1 piece	40
Struedel	1 average piece	200
Tart	1 med. piece	150
Tart, with Fruit Filling	1 med. piece	200

Pies

Apple	⅐th section	330
Apricot	⅐th section	330
Banana Cream	⅐th section	340
Berry (Most Flavors)	⅐th section	300
Blackberry	⅐th section	300
Blueberry	⅐th section	290
Butterscotch	⅐th section	265
Cheese	⅐th section	330
Cheesecake	1/12th of 12" diameter	300
Cherry	⅐th section	340
Coconut Custard	⅐th section	265
Custard Cream	⅐th section	265
Gooseberry	⅐th section	300
Lemon Chiffon	⅐th section	300
Lemon Meringue	⅐th section	300
Mince	⅐ section	365
Peach	⅐th section	330

Peach Cream	1/7th section	355
Pineapple	1/7th section	340
Pineapple Cheesecake	1/12th of 12" diameter	310
Pineapple Cheese Pie	1/7th section	340
Pineapple Cream Pie	1/7th section	350
Prune Whip Pie	1/7th section	330
Pumpkin	1/7th section	265
Raisin	1/7th section	325
Rhubarb	1/7th section	330
Strawberry	1/7th section	310
Strawberry Cream	1/7th section	350

Puddings

Apple Snow	1/2 cup (4 oz.)	75
Apricot Whip	1/2 cup (4 oz.)	100
Banana Custard	1/2 cup (4 oz.)	125
Banana Whip	1/2 cup (4 oz.)	85
Bread Pudding	1/2 cup (4 oz.)	150
Butterscotch Pudding	1/2 cup (4 oz.)	175
Caramel	1/2 cup (4 oz.)	170
Custards (Most Types)	1/2 cup (4 oz.)	150

Toppings, Dessert

Black Raspberry (Kraft)	1 T.	40
Butterscotch (Hershey's)	1 T.	55
Caramel (Smucker's)	1 T.	50
Chocolate Fudge (Hershey's)	1 T.	60
Hard Sauce	1 T.	65
Marshmallow Cream	1 T.	45
Pecans in Syrup	1 T.	90
Pineapple Syrup	1 T.	40
Strawberry Syrup	1 T.	50
Whipped Cream (Reddi Whip)	1 T.	10

DINING OUT AND PARTY FOODS

Cocktail Hour Appetizers

Seasoning and sauces are not added to calorie count unless mentioned. Adjust by adding calories for ingredients included in preparation.

Anchovy Canape	6 small fillets	65
Caviar (Most Types)	1 T.	35
Celery and Olives	2 stalks, 6 olives	70
Celery, Stuffed	2 med. stalks	75
Clams, Cherrystone	4 oz. of meat	90
Clams, Little Neck	4 oz. of meat	90
Clams, Steamers	4 oz. of meat	85
Corn Chips (Fritos)	1 oz.	165
Crab Meat, Canned	3 oz. portion	85

Crab Meat, Deviled	1 med. portion	200
Crab Meat, Fresh	3 oz. portion	90
Cream Cheese Spreads (Average)	1 oz.	95
Eggs, Stuffed	2 halves	125
Fruit, Canned	1/4 cup (6 oz.)	135
Fruit, Fresh	1/4 cup (6 oz.)	85
Gefilte Fish	1 piece	55
Ham, Prosciutto (or Others)	1 1/2 oz. portion	170
Herring, Kippered	4 oz. portion	240
Herring, Pickled	4 oz. portion	100
Herring in Sour Cream	4 oz. portion	240
Hors d'Oeuvres (Cold)	4 oz. portion	270
Hors d'Oeuvres (Hot)	4 oz. portion	310
Liver, Chicken (Chopped)	3 oz. portion	155
Lobster, Canned	3 oz. portion	80
Lobster, Fresh	3 oz. portion	75
Lox (Most Kinds)	3 oz. portion	285
Mushroom, Cocktail	3 oz. jar	20
Neufchatel Cheese Spread	1 oz.	70
Onion, Cocktail	1	trace
Oysters, Bluepoint	6 to 9 medium	100
Oysters, Cape Cod	5 to 8 medium	100
Paté	3 oz. portion	130 to 280
Popcorn (Unbuttered)	1 cup	145
Pretzels (Very Thin)	1 piece	1
Salami	4 thin slices	100
Salmon, Smoked	3 oz. portion	285
Sardines, with Oil	3 oz. portion	180
Sardines, with Tomato Sauce	3 oz. portion	110
Shad Roe	2 oz. portion	100
Shrimps, Canned (Drained)	3 oz.	75
Shrimps, Fresh	3 oz. (6 med.)	75
Snails Bourguignonne	6 med. size	100
Sturgeon, Smoked	2 1/2 oz. portion	100
Trout, Brook or Lake, Smoked	3 oz. portion	110
Tuna, Canned (Drained)	3 oz. portion	170
Tuna, Fresh	3 oz. portion	150
Tuna, Smoked	2 1/2 oz. portion	125
Vegetables, Raw (See Vegetables, page 141.)		

Appetizers Prepared

Cheese Straws, Frozen	1 piece	50
Franks in Blankets, Frozen	1 piece	55
Gefilte Fish Cocktail	1 piece	55
Herring in Sour Cream	2 oz.	120
Herring, Pickled	2 oz.	50
Meatballs, Cocktail, Canned	1 piece	10
Paté, with Herbs, Canned	1 oz.	75
Sausages, Cocktail, Canned	4 oz.	70
Shrimp Cocktail, with Sauce	4 1/2 oz. (5 med.)	155

DINNER SELECTIONS

Chinese Food

Beef Chop Suey	1 cup	150
Chicken Cantonese	1 cup	310
Chicken Chow Mein without Noodles	1 cup	115
Chinese Vegetables	1 cup	25
Chow Mein Noodles	1/2 cup	130
Egg Roll, Plain	1	50
Egg Roll, Shrimp	1	55
Fortune Cookie	1	35
Fried Rice, Chicken	1 cup	230
Fried Rice, Pork	1 cup	240
Fried Rice, Shrimp	1 cup	210
Shrimp Chow Mein without Noodles	1 cup	190
Tea (no Sugar)	1 cup	0

Fish and Seafood (see also page 132.)

Bluefish, Baked or Broiled	4 oz.	195
Bluefish, Fried in Butter	4 oz.	310
Clam Chowder, Manhattan	1 cup	90
Clam Chowder, New England	1 cup	210
Cole Slaw	1 cup	80
Crab Meat, Deviled	1 crab	200
Crackers, Oyster	10 small (3/4 lb)	90
Flounder, Broiled	6 oz.	120
Lobster, Whole, Broiled	1 small (3/4 lb)	90
Lobster, Creamed	1/2 cup	150
Oyster Stew	8 oz.	245
Red Snapper, Broiled	4 oz.	95
Swordfish, Broiled	3 oz.	150
Tartar Sauce	1 T.	70

Italian Food

Breadstick	1	40
Cheese (Grated)	1 T.	35
Italian Bread, (no Butter)	3/4" slice	80
Pizza:		
Cheese	9" diameter	800
Pepperoni	9" diameter	900
Sausage	9" diameter	1000
Deluxe	12" diameter	1750
Lasagna	1 portion (8 oz.)	340
Manicotti	1 piece	165
Spaghetti (Cooked)	1 cup	155
Spaghetti with Meat Sauce	1 cup	300
Spaghetti and Meat Balls	1 cup meatballs 1 cup spaghetti	360
Wine, Dry Red or White	4 oz.	95
Ice Cream, Spumoni	1/2 cup	285

Steak (see also page 130.)

Beef Rib Roast	3½ oz.	265
Hamburger, Chopped (Cooked)	3 oz.	245
Lamb Chops, Loin, Broiled (without Bone)	3½ oz.	225
Liver (Cooked)	4 oz.	260
Potato, Baked with Butter	1	140
Potato, Baked with Butter, Sour Cream, and Chives	1	260
Roast	3 oz.	375
Round	3½ oz.	280
Porterhouse	3½ oz.	245
Sirloin	3½ oz.	330
Swiss Steak	4″ × 1″ × ¾″	130
T-Bone	3½ oz.	250
Tenderloin	3½ oz.	225
Sweetbreads (Cooked)	4 oz.	100

Sauces (see also page 138.)

A-1 Sauce	1 T.	25
Catsup	1 T.	20
Horseradish	1 t.	1
Soy Sauce	1 T.	5
Worcestershire Sauce	1 T.	25

EGGS

Boiled (in the Shell)	1 med. (2 oz.)	80
Deviled	2 med. halves	125
Fried	1 med. (2 oz.)	100
Omelette	1 med. (2 oz.)	105
Poached	1 med. (2 oz.)	80
Scrambled	1 med. (2 oz.)	110
Stuffed	2 med. halves	125
White Only	1 med.	15
Yolk Only	1 med.	60

FATS AND OILS

Bacon	1 T.	100
Beef Drippings	1 T.	50
Butter, Salt and Sweet	1 T.	100
Chicken Fat	1 T.	100
Cod Liver Oil	1 T.	100
Corn Oil	1 T.	125
Crisco	1 T.	110
Fat, Vegetable	1 T.	110
Gravy (Thick)	1 T.	65
Gravy (Med. Thick)	1 T.	50
Lard	1 T.	125
Margarine	1 T.	100
Margarine, Diet	1 T.	

Calorie Counter / 127

Olive Oil	1 T.	125
Peanut Oil	1 T.	120
Safflower Oil	1 T.	105
Salad Oil	1 T.	125
Soybean Oil	1 T.	125

FRUITS

Apple (Medium)	2½" diameter	80
Apple (Small)	2¼" diameter	60
Apple, Baked (with Sugar)	3" diameter	160
Apple, Baked (no Sugar)	2½" diameter	75
Applesauce (Sweetened)	½ cup (4 oz.)	160
Applesauce, (Unsweetened)	½ cup (4 oz.)	50
Apricots, Canned in Syrup	4 med. halves and syrup	100
Apricots, Canned, Water-Packed	8 oz. cup halves	85
Apricots, Dried	8 oz. cup halves	400
Apricots, Fresh	3 med.	55
Apricots, Frozen	4 oz. serving	95
Apricots, Stewed (Sweetened)	8 oz. cup	400
Apricots, Stewed (Unsweetened)	8 oz. cup	245
Avocado	½ average	185
Bananas (Large)	8"	120
Bananas (Medium)	6"	90
Blackberries, Canned in Syrup	8 oz. cup	220
Blackberries, Canned in Water	8 oz. cup	105
Blackberries, Fresh	8 oz. cup	85
Blueberries, Canned in Syrup	8 oz. cup	245
Blueberries, Canned in Water	8 oz. cup	90
Blueberries, Fresh	8 oz. cup	85
Cantaloupe	½ of 5" diameter	60
Casaba Melon	2" × 9" wedge	55
Cherries, Canned	8 oz. cup	230
Cherries, Fresh	8 oz. cup	80
Cherries, Maraschino	1 med.	20
Coconut Milk	8 oz. cup	60
Coconut, Fresh	2" × 2" × ½" piece	160
Coconut, Shredded	8 oz. level cup	350
Crab Apple	1 med.	30
Cranberries	8 oz. cup	55
Cranberry Sauce (Sweetened)	8 oz. cup	550
Currants, Cooked with Sugar	8 oz. cup	125
Currants, Fresh	8 oz. cup	60
Figs, Canned in Syrup	3 figs; 2 T. syrup	130
Figs, Dried	1 large 2" × 1"	60
Figs, Fresh	3 small 1½" diameter	90
Fruit Cocktail, Canned in Syrup	8 oz. cup	195
Fruit Cocktail, Fresh	¾ cup (6 oz.)	85
Gooseberries	8 oz. cup	60
Grapes	40 med.	100
Grapefruit	½ large 5" diameter	55
Grapefruit, Canned (Sweetened)	8 oz. cup	180

128 / *Candy, Chocolate, Ice Cream and How to Lick 'em!*

Grapefruit, Canned (Unsweetened)	8 oz. cup	90
Grapefruit Sections	8 oz. cup	80
Guavas	3 oz. guava	50
Huckleberries	8 oz. cup	85
Kumquat	3 oz. piece	65
Lemon	2" × 2¾" oval	20
Lemon Juice	1 T.	5
Lemonade (Sugar Added)	8 oz. glass	100
Lichi Nuts	8 pieces (3½ oz.)	65
Loganberries, Canned	8 oz. cup	105
Loganberries, Fresh	8 oz. cup	90
Mangos (Medium)	7 oz.	90
Muskmelon	½ of 5" diameter	40
Nectarine	1 med.	40
Olives, Green	10 olives	75
Olives, Manzanilla (Ripe)	10 olives	75
Olives, Mission	10 olives	105
Olives, Stuffed	5 mammoth	55
Orange (Large)	3½" diameter	110
Orange (Medium)	3" diameter	75
Orange (Small)	2½" diameter	60
Orange Sections	8 oz. cup	90
Orange and Grapefruit Sections	8 oz. cup	85
Orange Juice, Canned (Sweetened)	8 oz. cup	135
Orange Juice, Canned (Unsweetened)	8 oz. cup	110
Papaya	8 oz. cup	70
Peach, Fresh	2½" × 2"	35
Peach, Fresh, Sliced	8 oz. cup	80
Peaches, Canned in Syrup	2 med. halves & lqd.	90
Peaches, Canned, Water Packed	8 oz. cup	65
Pear, Fresh	3" × 2½"	95
Pear, Fresh (Quartered)	8 oz. cup	120
Pear, Spiced	1 med.	80
Pears, Canned, in Syrup	2 med. halves and lqd.	90
Pears, Canned, Water Pack	8 oz. cup	80
Persian Melon	2" × 9" wedge	55
Persimmons (Seeded Type)	2¼" diameter	75
Persimmons (Seedless Type)	2¼" diameter	95
Pineapple, Canned in Syrup	2 small slices	100
Pineapple, Canned in Syrup	1 large slice	95
Pineapple, Crushed	8 oz. cup	205
Pineapple, Fresh, Diced	8 oz. cup	75
Pineapple, Fresh, Sliced	¾ × 3½" diameter	45
Plantain	3½ oz. portion	120
Plums, Canned in Syrup	3 prunes	95
Plums, Fresh	2" diameter	30
Pomegranate	1 average	75
Prickly Pear	1 average	55
Prunes, Dried (Large)	1¾" diameter × ¾"	25
Prunes, Dried (Medium)	1½" diameter × ½"	20

Prunes, Stewed (Sugar Added)	4 oz. (½ cup)	245
Prunes, Stewed (no Sugar)	4 oz. (½ cup)	155
Quince, Fresh	1 average	35
Raisins	1 T.	25
Raspberries, Canned	8 oz. cup	250
Raspberries, Fresh (Black)	8 oz. cup	100
Raspberries, Fresh (Red)	8 oz. cup	70
Raspberries, Frozen	10 oz. package	75
Rhubarb, Canned	8 oz. cup	385
Rhubarb, Fresh, Diced	8 oz. cup	20
Rhubarb, Stewed with Sugar	8 oz. cup	385
Strawberries, Fresh	8 oz. cup	55
Strawberries, Frozen	10 oz. package	310
Tangerine	2½" diameter med.	35
Tomatoes, Canned	8 oz. cup	45
Tomatoes, Fresh	2" × 2½" diameter med.	30
Tomatoes, Fresh	1¾" × 2¼" diameter small	25
Tomatoes, Stewed	8 oz. cup	50
Watermelon	½" slice, 10" diameter	45
Watermelon	4" × 8" wedge	120

JUICES

Apple, Canned	8 oz. glass	125
Apple, Fresh	8 oz. glass	125
Apricot Nectar	4 oz. glass	170
Blackberry	4 oz. glass	35
Blueberry	4 oz. glass	35
Carrot	4 oz. glass	25
Cider, Apple (Fermented)	8 oz. glass	95
Cider, Apple (Sweet)	8 oz. glass	115
Clam	4 oz. glass	45
Coconut Milk	8 oz. glass	60
Currant	4 oz. glass	55
Grape, Canned or Bottled	4 oz. glass	85
Grapefruit, Canned (Sweetened)	8 oz. glass	130
Grapefruit, Canned (Unsweetened)	8 oz. glass	90
Grapefruit, Fresh, Squeezed	8 oz. glass	90
Grapefruit, Frozen (Diluted)	6 oz. glass	85
Kraut	4 oz. glass	25
Lemon, Canned (Unsweetened)	1 T.	5
Lemonade (Sweetened)	8 oz. glass	100
Lime (Undiluted)	4 oz. glass	30
Loganberry	4 oz. glass	70
Nectarine	4 oz. glass	55
Orange, Canned Concentrate	8 oz. gl. diluted 1:7	35
Orange, Canned (Sweetened)	8 oz. glass	135
Orange, Canned (Unsweetened)	8 oz. glass	110
Orange, Fresh, Squeezed	8 oz. glass	110

Orange, Frozen Concentrate (Diluted)	8 oz. glass	100
Orange-Grapefruit, Canned (Unsweetened)	8 oz. glass	100
Orange-Grapefruit, Canned (Sweetened)	8 oz. glass	135
Orange-Grapefruit, Frozen Concentrate (Diluted)	8 oz. glass	105
Papaya	4 oz. glass	55
Papaya Juice Ade	8 oz. glass	70
Peach Nectar	4 oz. glass	65
Pear Nectar	4 oz. glass	50
Pineapple, Canned	4 oz. glass	60
Pomegranate	4 oz. glass	75
Prune	4 oz. glass	100
Raspberry	4 oz. glass	70
Sauerkraut	4 oz. glass	25
Tangerine, Canned (Unsweetened)	8 oz. glass	95
Tangerine, Fresh, Squeezed	4 oz. glass	50
Tomato	8 oz. glass	50
V-8 Cocktail	4 oz. glass	25
Vegetable	4 oz. glass	40

MEAT, FISH, SEAFOOD, AND POULTRY

Meat

Bacon, Broiled or Fried	2 average slices	100
Bacon, Canadian	4 oz. portion	265
Beef, Boiled	3 oz. portion	185
Beef, Chipped	8 oz. cup	340
Beef, Chipped and Creamed	1/2 cup (4 oz.)	175
Beef, Chuck (Cooked, without Bone)	3 1/2 oz.	420
Beef, Corned, Boiled	4" × 1 1/2" × 1" piece	100
Beef, Corned, Canned (Lean)	3 oz. portion	160
Beef, Corned, Canned (Fat)	3 oz. portion	195
Beef, Corned and Hashed	3 oz. portion	155
Beef, Flank (Cooked, without Bone)	3 1/2 oz.	235
Beef, Hamburger	3 oz. portion	245
Beef Heart	3 oz. portion	160
Beef Kidney	3 oz. portion	120
Beef Liver, Fried	2 oz. portion	130
Beef Lung	4 oz. portion	105
Beef, Porterhouse Steak (without Bone)	3 1/2 oz. portion	245
Beef, Pot Roast (Cooked)	3 1/2 oz. portion	300
Beef, Rib Roast (without Bone)	3 1/2 oz. portion	265
Beef, Round Steak (without Bone)	3 1/2 oz. portion	280
Beef, Rump Roast (without Bone)	3 oz. portion	375
Beef, Sirloin Steak (without Bone)	3 oz. portion	330
Beef Stew	8 oz. cup	350
Beef Sweetbreads	1/2 cup (4 oz.)	100
Beef, Swiss Steak	4" × 1" × 3/4" piece	130
Beef, T-Bone Steak (without Bone)	3 1/2 oz. portion	250
Beef, Tenderloin Steak	3 1/2 oz. portion	225

Beef Tongue, (Med. Fat)	4 oz. portion	235
Beef Tongue, Pickled	3 oz. portion	210
Beef Tripe	1/2 cup (4 oz.)	100
Beef and Vegetable Stew	8 oz. cup	255
Bologna	1 1/2" diameter × 1"	470
Brains (All animals)	3 oz. portion	105
Calves Brains	3 oz. portion	105
Calves Liver	3 oz. portion	120
Filet Mignon	3 1/2 oz. portion	225
Frankfurter	1 average (1 1/2 oz.)	155
Ham, Baked	4 1/4" × 4" × 1/2" slice	265
Ham, Boiled (without Bone)	3 1/2 oz. portion	340
Ham, Boiled, Luncheon Meat	2 oz. portion	175
Ham, Deviled	2 T.	100
Ham Hocks	3 oz. portion	340
Ham Loaf	3 oz. portion	355
Ham, Luncheon Meat, Boiled	2 oz.	135
Ham, Luncheon Meat, Spiced	2 oz. portion	165
Ham, Prosciutto	1 1/2 oz. portion	170
Ham, Smoked (with Bone)	3 1/2 oz. portion	325
Ham, Smoked (without Bone)	3 1/2 oz. portion	395
Head Cheese (Sausage)	3 oz. piece	70
Lamb Chops, Loin, Broiled (without Bone)	3 1/2 oz. portion	225
Lamb Chops, Rib, Broiled (without Bone)	3 1/2 oz. portion	295
Lamb, Roast, Leg (without Bone)	3 oz. portion	230
Lamb Liver	3 oz. portion	115
Lamb, Roast, Shoulder (without Bone)	3 oz. portion	285
Lamb, Sirloin Chops (with Bone)	2 1/2" × 1 1/2" × 3/4" piece	400
Lamb Stew	8 oz. cup	255
Liver Spread	2 T.	95
Liverwurst	2 oz. slice	150
Meat Balls	1 med. 3 oz.	320
Meat Loaf	1 slice, 3 oz.	220
Mutton, Chops or Roast (Lean)	3 1/2 oz. portion	240
Mutton, Chops or Roast (Med. Fat)	3 1/2 oz. portion	320
Pastrami	2 med. slices (2 oz.)	170
Pigs Feet, Boiled	4 oz. portion	185
Pigs Feet, Pickled	4 oz. portion	230
Pork, Canned, Spiced	2 oz. portion	165
Pork Chops (with Bone)	4 oz.	260
Pork Chops, Loin Cut (without Bone)	3 1/2 oz.	250
Pork, Cured Bacon (Fat)	3 1/2 oz., med.	630
Pork, Cured Ham (Fat)	3 oz., med.	345
Pork, Roast, Leg	3 oz. portion	270
Pork Liver	3 oz. portion	115
Pork Loin, Roasted	1 chop (3 1/2 oz)	295
Pork Loin, Roasted (without Bone)	3 oz. portion	285
Pork, Salt	3 1/2 oz. portion	240
Pork Sausage	4 oz. portion	540
Pork Sirloin	3 1/2 oz. portion	225
Pork, Spareribs	3 1/2 oz. portion	350

Pork Tenderloin	3½ oz. portion	240
Pork Tongue	3½ oz. portion	215
Rabbit	3½ oz. portion	160
Sausage, Bologana	1½" diameter × 1"	470
Sausage, Cervelat	2" diameter × ¼"	50
Sausage, Frankfurter	1 average (1½ oz.)	125
Sausage, Liverwurst	2 oz. slice	150
Sausage, Pork	4 oz. portion	540
Sausage, Pork Links	2 average	125
Sausage, Salami	1½" diameter × 1"	470
Sausage, Summer	2½" × 2½" × ¼" slice	50
Sausage, Vienna	4 oz. portion	250
Sheep, Liver	3 oz. portion	115
Sheep, Kidney	3 oz. portion	90
Sirloin Steak (with Bone)	4 oz. portion	205
Sirloin Steak (without Bone)	3½ oz. portion	190
Steer Liver	2 oz. portion	110
Sweetbreads, Broiled	½ cup. (4 oz.)	100
Sweetbreads, Creamed	½ cup (4 oz.)	300
Tongue	4 oz. portion	255
Tripe	4 oz. portion	100
Veal (Med. Fat)	3 oz. portion	230
Veal Chop	3½ oz. portion	210
Veal Cutlet, Breaded (without Bone)	2 oz. portion	185
Veal Cutlet, Broiled (without Bone)	3 oz. portion	180
Veal Kidneys	3 oz. portion	120
Veal Liver	3 oz. portion	120
Veal, Roast, Rump (without Bone)	4 oz. portion	200
Veal, Roast, Sirloin (without Bone)	3½ oz. portion	180
Veal Steak	4 oz. portion	235
Veal Stew	8 oz. cup	250
Vegetable and Beef Stew	8 oz. cup	250
Venison (Average Cut)	4 oz. portion	225
Vienna Sausage	4 oz. portion	250

Fish and Seafoods

Abalone, Broiled or Fresh	3½ oz. portion	110
Abalone, Canned	3½ oz. portion	80
Anchovies, Canned	6 small fillets	65
Anchovy Paste	1 T.	40
Bass, Baked or Broiled	4 oz. portion	180
Bluefish, Baked or Broiled	3 oz.	135
Bluefish, Fried in Butter	3 oz.	285
Butterfish, Baked or Broiled	3 oz. portion	175
Catfish, Baked or Broiled	3 oz. portion	170
Caviar	1 T.	35
Clam Juice	4 oz. glass	45
Clams, Canned	3 oz. meat and liquid	45
Clams, Cherrystone, Little Neck	4 oz. meat	90
Clams, Steamers	4 oz. meat	80
Cod, Baked or Broiled	3½ oz. portion	100

Food	Portion	Calories
Codfish Balls	2 small	75
Codfish Cakes	2½" diameter × ½"	125
Crab, Cracked	1 med.	95
Crab, Hard or Soft Shell	3½ oz. portion	90
Crabmeat, Canned	3 oz. meat	85
Crabmeat, Deviled	1 medium crab	200
Croaker, Baked or Broiled	4 oz. portion	110
Eel, Fresh Broiled	4 oz. portion	185
Eel, Smoked	4 oz. portion	185
Finnan Haddie	4 oz. portion	100
Flounder, Baked or Broiled	4 oz. portion	80
Frogs Legs	4 oz. portion	75
Gefilte Fish	4 oz. portion	75
Haddock, Baked or Broiled	4" × 3" × ½" fillet	160
Haddock, Creamed	4 oz. portion	150
Haddock, Fried	4" × 3" × ½" fillet	195
Haddock, Smoked	4 oz. portion	135
Halibut, Broiled or Baked	4" × 3" × ½" steak	230
Halibut, Creamed	4 oz. portion	170
Herring, Atlantic	4 oz. portion	220
Herring, Kippered	4 oz. portion	240
Herring, Lake	4 oz. portion	160
Herring, Pacific	4 oz. portion	105
Herring, Pickled	4 oz. portion	105
Lobster, Broiled	¾ lb.	90
Lobster, Canned	3 oz. portion	80
Lobster, Creamed	½ cup (4 oz.)	150
Lox, Smoked	3 oz. portion	285
Mackerel, Baked or Broiled	3 oz. portion	200
Mackerel, Canned	3 oz. portion	155
Mackerel, Salt	4 oz. portion	175
Mussels	6 med.	75
Oysters, Fried in Butter	5 med.	225
Oysters, Raw, Blue Point	6 to 9 med.	100
Oyster, Raw, Cape Cod	5 to 8 med.	100
Oyster Stew (with ½ Cream & Milk)	8 oz. cup	300
Oyster Stew (with Whole Milk)	8 oz. cup	245
Oyster Stew (with Skimmed Milk)	8 oz. cup	155
Perch, Baked or Broiled	3 oz. portion	195
Pickerel, Baked or Broiled	4 oz. portion	85
Pike, Baked or Broiled	4 oz. portion	85
Porgy, Baked or Broiled	4 oz. portion	110
Red Fish, Baked or Broiled	4 oz. portion	100
Red Snapper, Baked or Broiled	4 oz. portion	95
Salmon, Baked or Broiled	4" × 3" × ½" piece	205
Salmon	3 oz.	120
Salmon, Creamed	½ cup (4 oz.)	200
Salmon, Loaf	4" × 3" × ½" piece	200
Salmon, Smoked	3 oz. portion	285
Sardines in Oil (Drained)	3 oz. portion	180
Sardines in Oil	3 oz. portion	300

Sardines in Tomato Sauce	3 oz. portion	185
Scallops, Baked or Broiled	4 oz. portion	175
Scallops, Fried in Butter	3 to 5 med. pieces	295
Shad, Baked or Broiled	4 oz. portion	190
Shad Roe	2 oz. portion	100
Shrimps, Canned (Drained)	3 oz. portion	110
Shrimps, Fresh, Broiled	6 med. (3 oz.)	75
Shrimps, Fried, Sauteed	3½ oz. portion	285
Smelts, Baked or Broiled	2 small	50
Snails	6 med.	55
Sole, Fillet, Baked or Broiled	4 oz. portion	100
Squid, Fresh, Raw	3½ oz. portion	80
Sturgeon, Smoked	3½ oz. portion	100
Swordfish, Baked or Broiled	3 oz. portion	150
Trout, Brook, Baked or Broiled	3½ oz. portion	50
Trout, Brook, Smoked	3 oz. portion	100
Trout, Lake, Baked or Broiled	3 oz. portion	60
Trout, Lake, Smoked	3 oz. portion	110
Tuna, Baked or Broiled	3 oz. portion	150
Tuna, Canned	3 oz. drained	170
Tuna, Canned (with Oil)	3 oz. portion	250
Tuna, Smoked	2½ oz. portion	125
Turtle Meat	½ cup (4 oz.)	160
Whitefish, Baked or Broiled	4 oz. portion	125
Whitefish, Fried in Butter	4 oz. portion	280

Poultry

Chicken, à La King	½ cup (4 oz.)	220
Chicken, Boiled	3 oz. portion	75
Chicken Boiled (in Soup)	8 oz. cup	125
Chicken, Broiled (Boned)	½ med. (3 oz.)	115
Chicken, Canned (Boned)	3 oz. portion	170
Chicken, Creamed	½ cup (4 oz.)	220
Chicken Croquettes	1 med.	105
Chicken Fat	1 T.	100
Chicken Gizzards	3½ oz. portion	120
Chicken Hearts	3 oz. portion	135
Chicken Liver, Broiled	3½ oz. portion	140
Chicken Livers, Sauteed	3 oz. portion	155
Chicken Parts, Broiler (Boned)	½ bird (8 oz.)	335
Chicken Parts, Fryers (Boned)	1 breast (8 oz.)	210
Chicken Parts, Fryers (Boned)	1 leg (8 oz.)	160
Chicken Parts, Roasters (Boned)	4 oz. piece	230
Chicken Parts, Stewing Hen (Boned)	4 oz. piece	345
Duck, Roasted (Boned)	4 oz. piece	325
Goose, Roasted (Boned)	4 oz. piece	315
Liver, Chopped, Chicken	3 oz. portion	150
Paté (Recipe Varies)	3 oz. portion	130 to 280
Pheasant, Roasted (Boned)	3 oz. portion	150
Quail, Broiled	4 oz. portion	150
Squab, Broiled (Boned)	3 oz. portion	280

Stuffing, (Meat or Poultry)	1/4 cup (2 oz.)	110
Turkey, Dark Meat (Boned)	4 oz. portion	330
Turkey, White Meat (Boned)	4 oz. portion	280
Turkey Gizzard	3 1/2 oz. portion	190
Turkey, Roasted	4 oz. portion	320

NATURAL AND ORGANIC FOODS

Also See Fruits, Juices, Nuts and Seeds, and Vegetables

Beverages

Coffee Substitute (Dina-Mite)	1 cup brewed	5

Fruits See Page 127.

Candy

Coconut Bar (Lind)	1-1.2 oz. bar	170
Honey Nut Bar (Lind)	1-1.2 oz. bar	150
Nut Bar with Currants (Lind)	1-1.2 oz. bar	140
Nut Bar with Ghia (Lind)	1-1.2 oz. bar	150
Pecasheo Bar (Lind)	1-1.2 oz. bar	160
Pignolia Nut Bar (Lind)	1-1.2 oz. bar	170
Sesame Nut Bar (Lind)	1-1.2 oz. bar	170
Yinnies, Macrobiotic Candy Kisses (Chico-San)	1 piece	20

Grains and Powders

Cereal (Dina-Mite) Whole Wheat, Bran, Wheat Germ, and Flax (Uncooked)	1 oz.	100
Cracked Wheat, Kinslow's Wheat Nuts, (Uncooked)	1 oz.	100
Granola	1 oz.	135
Kasha Buckwheat Groats Wolff's (Cooked)	1 cup	290
Powerhouse 32 (Vita Foods)	1/4 cup	110
Protein, Liquid (Predigested) LPP	1 T.	20
Protein Supplement (Fearn Muscle Protein)	1/4 cup	105
Soya Bean Granules (Fearn)	1/4 cup	110
Soya Bean Pancake & Waffle Mix (Fearn)	1 oz.	120
Soya Bean Powder, High Lecithin (Fearn)	1 t.	115
Soya Bean Powder, Low-Fat (Fearn)	1 t.	10
Soya Bean Powder, Natural (Fearn)	1 t.	10
Wheat Germ	1 t.	40

Juices see page 129.

Macrobiotic Foods

Beverage/Cereal, Koko Grain (Chico-San)	¼ cup	60
Candy Kisses, Yinnies, (Chico-San)	1 piece	20
Cereal, Rice, Organic Brown Rice Base (Chico-San)	¼ cup	60
Koko Grain, Cereal/Beverage (Chico-San)	¼ cup	60
Macaroni, Organically Grown Buckwheat (Chico-San)	1 oz.	35
Macaroni, Organically Grown Whole-wheat (Chico-San)	1 oz.	35
Rice, Brown, Organic (Chico-San, (Cooked)	¼ cup	60
Rice Cakes, Organic Rice, Salted Plain (Chico-San)	1 cracker	35
Rice Cakes, Organic Rice, Unsalted, Plain (Chico-San)	1 cracker	30
Rice Cakes, Organic Rice, Salted Flavored with Whole Buckwheat or Millet (Chico-San)	1 cracker	30
Rice Cakes, Organic Rice, Unsalted Flavored with Whole Buckwheat or Millet (Chico-San)	1 cracker	30
Rice Cakes, Organic Rice (Spiral Foods)	1 cracker	30
Rice Cereal, Organic Brown Rice Base (Chico-San, Cooked)	¼ cup	60
Rice Chips, (Chico-San)	1 oz.	110
Soybean Paste, Miso (Chico-San)	1 T.	20
Soy Sauce, Tamari (Chico-San)	1 oz.	20
Spaghetti, Organically Grown Buckwheat (Chico-San)	1 oz.	35
Spaghetti, Organically Grown Whole-wheat (Chico-San)	1 oz.	35

Miscellaneous

Cracker, Akmak	1 piece	20
Sugar, Raw	1 t.	20
Honey	1 T.	65
Molasses, Blackstrap	1 T.	45
Yeast	1 T.	25

Nuts and Seeds See Page 137.

Vegetables

Beans Soy, Immature	1 cup	120
Beans, Soy, Mature Whole also See Page 141.	1 cup	695

NUTS AND SEEDS

Almonds, in Shell	1 cup	240
Almonds, Shelled	1/2 cup	425
Brazil Nuts, in Shell	1 cup (14 nuts)	395
Brazil Nuts, Shelled	1/2 cup (16 kernels)	455
Butternuts	5 to 6 average nuts	100
Cashew Nuts, Roasted	1/2 cup	380
Chestnuts, Roasted	3 1/2 oz.	190
Coconut Meat	1 cup	335
Coconut, Shredded, Dry	8 oz. cup	340
Filberts, Shelled	1 cup	905
Hazelnuts	8 to 10 average	100
Hickory	12 to 15 nuts	100
Lichi Nuts, Fresh	3 1/2 oz.	65
Lichi, Shelled, Dried	3 1/2 oz.	280
Lotus Seets	3 1/2 oz.	350
Peanuts, Chopped	1 T.	50
Peanuts, in Shell	12 to 15 nuts	100
Peanuts, Shelled	1 cup	840
Peanuts, Spanish	1/4 cup	240
Pecans	1 cup of halves	740
Pecans, Chopped	1 T.	55
Pine Nuts	12 to 15 nuts	100
Pistachio Nuts	12 average nuts	100
Pumpkin Seeds	3 1/2 oz.	445
Seasame Seeds, Whole	3 1/2 oz.	570
Sunflower Seeds, Shelled	3 1/2 oz.	180
Sunflower Seeds, in Shell	1 cup	550
Walnuts, Black	11 halves	100
Walnuts, Black, Chopped	1 T.	50
Walnuts, English	1 cup of halves	655
Walnuts, English, Chopped	1 T.	50
Walnuts, Persian	1 cup of halves	650
Walnuts, Persian, Chopped	1 T.	50

PREPARED FOODS

Appetizers, Prepared

Cheese Straws, Frozen	1 piece	50
Franks in Blankets, Frozen	1 piece	55
Gefilte Fish Cocktail	1 piece	55
Herring in Sour Cream	2 oz.	120
Herring, Pickled (Vita)	2 oz.	55
Meatballs, Cocktail, Canned	1 piece	10
Paté, with Herbs, Canned	1 oz.	75
Pizza, Cheese	2 1/2 oz.	165
Sausages, Cocktail, Canned	4 oz.	70
Shrimp Cocktail	4 1/2 oz.	155
Shrimp, with Cocktail Sauce	4 oz.	40

Meats

Beef, Sliced in Gravy, Frozen	5 oz. pkg.	160
Hash, Corned Beef, Canned	1 cup	430
Meatballs, in Gravy, Canned	1 cup	380
Salisbury Steak, in Gravy, Canned	12¾ oz.	835
Stew, Beef	1 cup	350

Fish and Seafood

Clams, Whole, Canned	½ cup	100
Codfish, Breaded, Frozen	11 oz. pkg.	335
Crab, Canned	7½ oz.	220
Crab, Cakes, Precooked, Frozen	6 oz. pkg.	495
Crab, Deviled, Frozen	6 oz. pkg.	375
Fish Roe, Canned	8 oz.	140
Seafood Croquettes with Newburg Sauce, Frozen	12 oz. pkg.	565
Shrimp, with Cocktail Sauce	4 oz.	40
Sole in Lemon Butter, Frozen	9 oz. pkg.	305

Poultry

Chicken, Canned (Boned)	5½ oz.	270
Chicken à la King, Canned	1 cup	240
Chicken Cacciatore, Breast, Frozen	7 oz. pkg.	250
Chicken Pot Pie, Frozen	8 oz. pie	415
Turkey, with Giblet Gravy, Frozen	5 oz. pkg.	130
Turkey Pot Pie, Frozen	1 average	400

TV Dinners

Beef	11 oz.	350
Beef, Chopped	11.2 oz.	425
Chicken Cantonese	11 oz.	305
Enchilada, Beef	12.4 oz.	465
Ham	10.3 oz.	360
Italian	11.2 oz.	415
Macaroni and Cheese	12.4 oz.	375
Meat Loaf	11.2 oz.	425
Salisbury Steak	11.2 oz.	400
Shrimp	7¾ oz.	370

SEASONINGS, SAUCES AND DRESSINGS

A-1 Sauce	1 T.	25
Barbecue Sauce, Bottled	½ cup	120
Boiled Dressing	1 T.	30
Blue Cheese Dressing	1 T.	75
Catsup, Tomato	1 T.	20
Chicory	10 small leaves	5
Chili Con Carne (Powder)	1 T.	30
Chili Sauce	1 T.	20
Clam Sauce, Red (La Rosa)	½ cup	90
Cranberry Sauce	3 T.	70
Cream Dressing (or Sauce)	1 T.	35

Creole Sauce	1 T.	25
French Dressing	1 T.	60
Fruit Gelatin Dressing	2 T.	15
Garlic	1 clove	5
Garlic Sauce (with Butter)	1 T.	100
Gravy (Med. Thick)	1 T.	50
Gravy, Beef, Canned	½ cup	60
Hard Sauce	1 T.	45
Hollandaise Sauce	1 T.	100
Horseradish	1 T.	1
Hot Sauce	½ t.	trace
Lemon	½ med. (2" dia)	10
Mayonnaise	1 T.	95
Mayonnaise, Commercial Type	1 T.	60
Mayonnaise Diet Dressing	1 T.	35
Miracle Whip	1 T.	55
Mustard	1 t.	10
Oils (Salad or Cooking)	1 T.	125
Oleomargarine	1 T.	100
Olive Oil	1 T.	110
Peanut Butter	1 T.	95
Peanut Oil	1 T.	110
Peppers, Hot Chili	1 pepper	trace
Pepper, Seasoned	½ t.	10
Plum Pudding Sauce	1 T.	100
Relish, Pickle:		
Hamburger	1 T.	20
Hot Dog	1 T.	25
India	1 T.	25
Sweet	1 T.	25
Relish with Mustard (Chow-Chow)	1 T.	5
Roquefort Dressing	1 T.	100
Russian Dressing	1 T.	110
Salad Dressing	1 T.	35
Salad Dressings, Bottled:		
Caesar	1 T.	70
French (Kraft)	1 T.	65
Garlic French	1 T.	70
Green Goddess (Wishbone)	1 T.	80
Italian (Kraft)	1 T.	80
Russian (Wishbone)	1 T.	75
Simple Syrup Sauce	1 T.	100
Sour Cream Sauce	2 T.	115
Soy Sauce	1 T.	5
Spaghetti Sauce	½ cup	90
Tartar Sauce	1 T.	70
Thousand Island Diet Dressing	1 T.	50
Thousand Island Dressing	1 T.	100
Tomato Sauce	1 T.	5
Vinegar	1 T.	5
White Sauce	1 T.	30
Wine Sauce	1 T.	20

140 / Candy, Chocolate, Ice Cream and How to Lick 'em!

Worcestershire Sauce	1 T.	25

SOUPS

Most Creamed Soups	8 oz. bowl	200
Most Clear Soups	8 oz. bowl	15
Asparagus, Cream of	8 oz. cup or bowl	200
Barley	8 oz. cup or bowl	120
Bean, Navy	8 oz. cup or bowl	190
Beef Broth	8 oz. cup or bowl	100
Beef, Cream of	8 oz. cup or bowl	205
Bouillon, Clear	8 oz. cup or bowl	10
Bouillon Cube	$1/2''$ to $3/4''$ cube	5
Celery, Cream	8 oz. cup or bowl	200
Chicken Broth	8 oz. cup or bowl	50
Chicken, Cream of	8 oz. cup or bowl	200
Chicken Gumbo	8 oz. cup or bowl	155
Chicken and Matzoh Balls	1 cup with 2 balls	200
Chicken Noodle	8 oz. cup or bowl	100
Chicken and Rice	8 oz. cup or bowl	100
Clam Chowder	8 oz. cup or bowl	90
Consomme, Clear	8 oz. cup or bowl	10
Corn Chowder, Cream of	8 oz. cup or bowl	200
Corn, Cream of	8 oz. cup or bowl	200
Creamed Soups (Most)	8 oz. cup or bowl	200
Duck, Cream of	8 oz. cup or bowl	210
Gumbo Creole	8 oz. cup or bowl	100
Lentil	8 oz. cup or bowl	110
Mock Turtle	8 oz. cup or bowl	165
Mulligatawny	8 oz. cup or bowl	150
Mushroom, Cream of	8 oz. cup or bowl	200
Mutton	8 oz. cup or bowl	110
Mutton Cream of	8 oz. cup or bowl	195
Navy Bean	8 oz. cup or bowl	190
Noodle	8 oz. cup or bowl	120
Onion, Cream of	8 oz. cup or bowl	200
Onion, French	8 oz. cup or bowl	125
Oxtail	8 oz. cup or bowl	150
Oyster Stew ($1/2$ Cream and Milk)	8 oz. cup or bowl	200
Oyster Stew (with Milk 1:1)	8 oz. cup or bowl	245
Oyster Stew (with Milk 1:3)	8 oz. cup or bowl	210
Oyster Stew (Skimmed Milk)	8 oz. cup or bowl	155
Pea	8 oz. cup or bowl	140
Pea, Cream of	8 oz. cup or bowl	205
Pepperpot	8 oz. cup or bowl	175
Potato	8 oz. cup or bowl	185
Potato, Cream of	8 oz. cup or bowl	215
Rice	8 oz. cup or bowl	120
Scotch Broth	8 oz. cup or bowl	100
Spinach, Cream of	8 oz. cup or bowl	205
Split Pea	8 oz. cup or bowl	140
Split Pea, Cream of	8 oz. cup or bowl	205

Tomato	8 oz. cup or bowl	90
Tomato, Cream of	8 oz. cup or bowl	200
Tomato, Puree	8 oz. cup or bowl	90
Vegetable	8 oz. cup or bowl	85
Vegetable and Beef	8 oz. cup or bowl	180

VEGETABLES

The calories listed for fresh vegetables also apply to frozen vegetables as long as no sauces have been added. For calorie content of Vegetable Juices see "Juices" on page 129.

Arrowroot	3½ oz. portion	125
Artichokes	4 hearts	20
Asparagus, Canned (Drained)	6 spears	20
Asparagus, Canned (Drained)	1 cup spears	40
Asparagus, Fresh or Frozen	1 cup spears	40
Bamboo Shoots	3½ oz. portion	30
Beans, Baked (Pork & Molasses)	8 oz. cup	325
Beans, Baked (Pork & Tomato)	8 oz. cup	295
Beans, Kidney, Canned	8 oz. cup	230
Beans, Kidney, Dried	3½ oz. portion	340
Beans, Lima, Canned (with Liquid)	1 cup	175
Beans, Lima, Canned (with Liquid) (Drained)	1 cup	155
Beans, Lima, Dried	½ cup	305
Beans, Lima, Fresh or Frozen	8 oz. cup	155
Beans, Navy, Dried	½ cup	320
Beans, Pea, Dried	½ cup	320
Beans, Snap Green, Canned (Drained)	1 cup	45
Beans, Snap Green, Canned (with Liquid)	1 cup	45
Beans, Snap Green, Fresh or Frozen	1 cup	30
Beans, Soy, Immature	1 cup	120
Beans, Soy, Whole-Mature	1 cup	695
Beans, String, Fresh	3½ oz. portion	35
Beans, Wax, Canned (with Liquid)	1 cup	45
Beans, Wax, Canned (Drained)	1 cup	30
Beans, Wax, Fresh	3½ oz. portion	35
Beans, White Marrow, Dried	½ cup	325
Beans, Yellow, Canned (Drained)	1 cup	30
Beans, Yellow, Canned (with Liquid)	1 cup	45
Beans, Yellow, Fresh or Frozen	3½ oz. portion	35
Beansprouts	½ cup	15
Beet Greens	1 packed cup	40
Beets, Canned (Drained)	1 cup	65
Beets, Canned (with Liquid)	1 cup	85
Beets, Fresh (Cooked)	1 cup	50
Beets, Pickled	1 cup	60
Broccoli, Fresh or Frozen	1 cup of stalks	45
Brussels Sprouts	1 cup	45
Cabbage, Celery (Cooked)	1 cup	30
Cabbage, Chinese (Cooked)	1 cup	30

142 / *Candy, Chocolate, Ice Cream and How to Lick 'em!*

Cabbage, Fresh, Shredded	1 cup	25
Cabbage, Fresh	1 wedge 3½″×4½″	25
Cabbage, Fresh, Boiled	1 cup	40
Calabash	3½ oz. portion	20
Carrots, Canned, Diced (Drained)	1 cup	45
Carrots, Canned, Diced (with Liquid)	1 cup	70
Carrots, Fresh, Diced (Cooked)	1 cup	45
Carrots, Fresh, Raw	1 carrot 5½″×1″	20
Carrots, Fresh, Raw (Grated)	1 cup	45
Cauliflower	1 cup	30
Cauliflower Buds	1 cup	25
Celeriac	8 to 14 roots	90
Celery, Diced (Cooked)	1 cup	25
Celery, Diced Fresh	1 cup	20
Celery, Fresh (Inner Stalks)	3 small stalks	10
Celery, Fresh (Outer Stalk)	1 large stalk	10
Chard	1 cup	30
Chard Leaves (Cooked)	1 cup	50
Chick Peas (Garbanzos) Dry	1 cup	755
Chives	3½ oz. portion	45
Collards	1 cup	75
Coriander	3½ oz. portion	40
Corn, Canned (Drained)	1 cup	140
Corn, Canned (with Liquid)	1 cup	170
Corn, Fresh	1¾″ diameter ×5″	85
Corn, Fresh, Kernels	1 cup	140
Corn, Popping, Kernels, Dry	1 cup	55
Cow Peas (Cooked)	1 cup	175
Cow Peas, Dry	1 cup mature seeds	755
Cress, Garden (Cooked)	1 cup	185
Cress, Garden, Fresh	4 oz. portion	50
Cucumber	2″ diameter × 7½″	25
Dandelion Greens (Cooked)	1 cup	60
Egg Plant	3½ oz. portion	25
Fennel Leaves	3½ oz. portion	30
Garbanzos (Chick Peas) Dry	1 cup	755
Garlic	1 clove	5
Ginger Root	3¼ portion	50
Kale, Cooked	8 oz. cup	30
Kahlrabi	8 oz. cup	50
Lentils, Split (without Seed Coat)	3½ oz.	340
Lentils, Whole Seeds	3½ oz.	340
Lettuce	2 lg. or 4 sml leaves	10
Lettuce, Head	1 lb.	70
Mung Bean Sprouts	8 oz. cup	20
Mushrooms, Button	3½ oz. portion	20
Mushrooms, Canned (with Liquid)	1 cup	40
Mushrooms, Fresh, Sliced	1 cup	20
Mustard Greens	1 packed cup	30
Okra	3½ oz. portion	35
Olives, Green	10 olives (2½ oz.)	75

Olives, Ascaiano (Ripe)	10 olives (2½ oz.)	70
Olives, Manzanilla (Ripe)	10 olives (2½ oz.)	75
Olives, Mission (Ripe)	10 olives (2½ oz.)	105
Olives, Sevilano (Ripe)	10 olives (2½ oz.)	70
Olives, Stuffed, Mammoth	5 olives (1½ oz.)	55
Onions, Boiled	1 cup	80
Onions, Creamed	½ cup (4 oz.)	110
Onions, Fried (in Oil)	½ cup (4 oz.)	165
Onions, Green (Raw)	6 small (1¾ oz.)	25
Onions, Raw (Mature)	1 T.	5
Onions, Raw (Bermuda)	2½" diameter (3¾ oz.)	50
Onions, Spanish	1 med.	10
Onions, Stewed	½ cup (4 oz.)	50
Parsley, Chopped	1 T.	1
Parsnips, Cooked	1 cup	95
Peas, Fresh, Garden, Shelled	3½ oz.	100
Peas, Fresh, Sugar, Podded	3½ oz.	55
Peas, Green, Canned (Drained)	8 oz. cup	145
Peas, Green, Canned (with Liquid)	8 oz. cup	170
Peas, Green, Split, Dry	1 cup	690
Peas, Green, Mature, Whole Dry	1 cup	680
Peppers, Green Fresh	1 med. (2½ oz.)	20
Peppers, Red, Hot	1 med. (2½ oz.)	20
Peppers, Stuffed (with Meat)	1 med.	185
Pickles, Bread and Butter	22 to 24 small	120
Pickles, Bread and Butter	6 average ¼" × 1½ diameter	30
Pickles, Dill	1¾" diameter × 4" long	15
Pickles, Sour	1¾" diameter × 4" long	15
Pickles, Sweet	¾" dia. × 2" long	15
Pickles, Sweet Mixed	1 T.	15
Pickles, Sweet, Mixed	1 cup of mixed	225
Pimentos	1 average (1¼ oz.)	10
Potato Chips	10 average 2" diameter	115
Potato Chips	7 large 3" diameter	110
Potatoes	1 large (3½ oz.)	85
Potatoes, Au Gratin	½ cup (4 oz.)	250
Potatoes, Baked (Unpeeled)	1 med. 2½ diameter	100
Potatoes, Boiled (Peeled)	1 med. 2½" diameter	105
Potatoes, Boiled, Diced (Peeled)	8 oz. cup	105
Potatoes, Boiled (Unpeeled)	1 med. 2½ diameter	180
Potatoes, Canned (Drained)	3 to 4 small	120
Potatoes, Canned (with Liquid)	8 oz. cup	145
Potatoes, Creamed	8 oz. cup	250
Potatoes, Escalloped	½ cup (4 oz.)	120
Potatoes, French Fried	8 pieces 2" × ½" square	160
Potatoes, Hashed Brown	8 oz. cup	470
Potatoes, Mashed (with Milk)	8 oz. cup	125
Potatoes, Steamed	1 med. 2½ diameter	105
Potatoes, Steamed, Diced	8 oz. cup	105
Potatoes, Sweet, Baked (Peeled)	5"×2" diameter	185
Potatoes, Sweet, Boiled (Peeled)	5"×2½" diameter	255

144 / Candy, Chocolate, Ice Cream and How to Lick 'em!

Potatoes, Sweet, Candied	1 sml. 3½" × 2¼"	315
Potatoes, Sweet, Canned	8 oz. cup	235
Pumpkin	3½ oz. portion	30
Pumpkin, Canned	8 oz. cup	80
Radishes	4 sml. (1½ oz.)	5
Radishes, Chinese	3½ oz. portion	20
Rice, Brown, Dry	8 oz. cup	350
Rice, Converted (Cooked)	8 oz. cup	205
Rice, Fried (Chinese Style)	8 oz. cup	260
Rice, Precooked, Dry	8 oz. cup	420
Rice, Spanish (Average Recipe)	8 oz. cup	300
Rice, White, Boiled	8 oz. cup	200
Rice, White, Dry	8 oz. cup	400
Rice, Wild, Boiled	8 oz. cup	275
Rice, Wild, Dry	8 oz. cup	600
Romaine	2 lg. or 4 sml. leaves	10
Rhubarb, Canned	8 oz. cup	385
Rhubarb, Fresh, Diced	8 oz. cup	20
Rhubarb (Sugar Added)	8 oz. cup	385
Rutabagas	8 oz. cup	50
Sauerkraut, Canned (Drained)	8 oz. cup	35
Sauerkraut, Canned (with Liquid)	8 oz. cup	45
Scallions	4 average	10
Soybean Sprouts	½ cup (4 oz.)	50
Spinach, Canned (Drained)	8 oz. cup	50
Spinach, Canned (with Liquid)	8 oz. cup	45
Spinach, Fresh, Cooked	8 oz. cup	50
Spinach, Fresh	4 oz. cup	25
Squash, Rhubarb	½ cup (4 oz.)	50
Squash, Summer	8 oz. cup	35
Squash, Winter, Baked, Mashed	8 oz. cup	130
Squash, Winter, Boiled, Mashed	8 oz. cup	90
Succatash	½ cup (4 oz.)	70
Swamp Cabbage	3½ oz. portion	30
Tomato, Raw (Small)	1¾" × 2¼" oval diameter	30
Tomatoes, Canned	8 oz. cup	50
Tomatoes, Stewed	8 oz. cup	50
Tomato Paste	6 oz.	185
Turnip Greens (Cooked)	½ cup (4 oz.)	50
Turnips, Diced (Cooked)	8 oz. cup	45
Turnips, Mashed (Cooked)	8 oz. cup	60
Watercress, Leaves and Stems	1 lb.	85
Yams, Baked (Peeled)	5" × 2"	185
Yams, Candied	1 sml. 3½" × 2¼"	315
Yams, Canned	8 oz. cup	235
Zucchini	½ cup (4 oz.)	25